M000079487

The Holy Book of Luck

ISBN: 978-1-5272-9765-4
London - UK

https://www.as-alzein.com
E-mail: contact@as-alzein.com

THE HOLY BOOK OF LUCK

What is luck?
Is it blind invisible force? Or rational energy with purpose?
Is hard work enough to be successful?

A. SAED ALZEIN

A. Saed Alzein

To the Soul of my first love…… My Mother

To the Soul of my first teacher…My Father

To the immortal adoration in my life……. my soulmate until the last light

To the four chambers of my heart….my children

Truth is a free treasure, yet no one can own it

A.   Saed Alzein

Contents

Preface

Preface

I have been fascinated by luck and chance since early childhood. I survived a traumatic car accident at the age of six and still remember being rushed to hospital covered in blood; my mother holding my hand. I could hear her heart beating frantically, worried that I wouldn't make it. Luckily, I did make it – I survived. Looking back at those days, I wonder if I can describe myself as lucky? Does being alive and in good health mean that you are lucky?

I grew up hearing people being called lucky. Some were lucky because they were rich, others by being in a happy and successful marriage/relationship, or by winning prizes and competitions. I watched people winning the lottery on their first try, while so many others did not win even when they were buying tickets and playing for years and years! I have always wondered what guides the flip of a coin. Were rich people born under a lucky star? Are we born lucky or unlucky? Is luck engineered by a higher power? I have read stories of people accidentally missing a doomed plane; stories of people investing a large sum of money in a successful company just before it went bankrupt - losing a life-breaking money; while others withdrew their investment just a few days before the same company collapsed.

Is luck the reason why some of us studied for that end-of-semester exam the night before and managed to pass with flying colours with minimum effort? Or the reason why you just managed to pick the right numbers for that Saturday night lotto draw? To some people, it may seem "supernatural" but just how out of the ordinary is it to be lucky?

What is luck exactly? Is it blind force that hits randomly and changes people's lives for the better or worse? Is it rational energy with conscious purpose? Does God or the universe dedicate where luck shall go? Can we harness luck as we do with wind and solar power? Answering these questions means finding the answers to intriguing mystery that have puzzled the greatest minds throughout the ages.

In this book, I am challenging the outdated notion that hard work is the only way to success. It is not.

You could work as hard as you can for as long as you are able, and still fail. You could be a faithful, loving, and extremely caring person yet still fail to find true love. We don't hear any stories of failure; we only hear stories of success and hard work because they are the exception and not the rule. I am trying to get you to think about luck from a deeper perspective. After years of reading, researching, and indeed working recently within a luck-based business, I am trying to shed some light on this very fascinating subject; hoping it will entertain you, make you wonder and think about one of the world's biggest mysteries: luck.

Chapter 1

Luck Throughout History

Luck Throughout History

Luck looks like a golden thread running through the fabric of history, bringing together ancient gods, gamblers, philosophers, theologians, emperors, scholars, and slaves. Through the ages, humanity has employed all its ability, imagination, and knowledge to dismantle luck in an effort to bring good or to avoid bad. There are many theological myths about luck as an interpreter of predestination, and entire philosophical movements were developed to deal with its dominance, and new branches and applications of mathematics arose to analyse it. Generations of astrologers and fortune-tellers earned their living and profited from trading in it, *but we have not yet succeeded in our hereditary struggle to domesticate or conquer this stubborn beast.*

Luck is a powerful word that is clouded in mystery and has been the centre of fascination since the dawn of civilization. The word luck itself is Middle Dutch in origin, according to Mental Floss. The word comes from 'luc', a shortening of 'gheluc', meaning "happiness or good fortune". The word was probably introduced into the English language in the 15th century as a gambling term.

Many polytheistic religions have specific gods or goddesses that are associated with luck, including Fortuna and Felicitas in the Ancient Roman religion (related to the words "fortunate" and "unfortunate" in English), Dedun the god of wealth and prosperity in Nubian religion, the Seven Lucky Gods in Japanese mythology, mythical American serviceman

John Frum in Polynesian cargo cults, and the inauspicious Lakshmi in Hinduism.

Through the lens of history, human beings for the most part have been incredibly superstitious and curious creatures. Warding off evil spirits started way before any Harry Potter book hit the shelf; it has been around since the dawn of human existence. Whether it was the earliest humans clothed in deer skins dancing frantically around an open fire or a present-day soothsayer who claims to be able to predict the next five years of your life, the concept of luck is enough to turn heads at the least.

Puzzled by the strange events associated with luck, many people have dared to unravel this vast mystery with a plethora of possible answers. Alfred Mele explored the problem of present luck and delved into the topic of free will and moral responsibility.[1]

The problem of present luck may not sound familiar, but it is simply an idea stemming from libertarian theories of free will which states that someone acting in a particular way or not is strictly tied down to luck.

Tying responsibility to luck might sound strange to some people, but attributing luck to some of our past decisions is plausible to others. Even if luck plays a part in decision making, it is certain that the consequences of such actions will affect the way decisions are made in the future. Luck may affect our future in one form or another, but looking back in history, how did we get to the stage we are at today? With the numerous cultures that grace this planet, the differences in opinion as to what luck means is sure to be as vast as the Pacific Ocean. So, let us navigate history as a compass to guide us through the development of the concept of luck over the centuries.

Anthropologists have provided us with many useful and interesting facts to give us insight into early human life and belief systems, for example, early cave writings showing that humans had the intention of protecting themselves from bad luck. To us, these may look like meaningless scribbles on a wall but to civilizations back then, they were powerful traditions. Powerful in the sense that it actually worked for them, though it may be hard for us to comprehend.

Even in modern times, you may come across a magic trick that just seemed too perfect to be true. Or maybe a friend just bought a Ouija board and swore that they saw something levitating in mid-air. To people who have experienced strange events, it just isn't something that can be reasoned away easily. Luck is similar, and as much as we attempt to find the 'best' explanation, it is most likely an impossible task. If some events are unexplainable today, then there are definitely similar natured events that happened in the past that science will have a hard time explaining. History is full of interesting facts, some of which imply that our present-day generation may actually be the boring lot compared to what the ancients got up to!

Luck and Kamikaze

On the 7th of March 1269; 17th September 1269; September 1271 and May 1272 AD Kublai Khan an ambitious emperor of the Mongol empire sent emissaries to the Japanese emperor demanding for Japan to become a vassal state and pay tribute under a threat of conflict. The emperor of Japan was not intimidated by the threats from Kublai Khan and in 1274 AD, 20 000 Mongolian soldiers and 500 ships marched on Japan, sure that they had smelled victory from afar.[2]

These troops wrecked the islands of Iki and Tsushima before finally reaching the shores of Hakata Bay in Japan. It was desperate times, and it didn't look good for the Japanese who had not fought on home soil for quite some time. Then magic struck! The Mongols' beaching attempt came to a complete halt due to a storm stretching as far as the eye could see. It tore through the Mongol army violently, leaving only a handful of boats floating on the surface but no survivors graced its waters. That famous incident in history was considered as luck playing its finest role in full force and it was from this event that the term 'Kamikaze' was born, the divine wind.

Less than ten years later the Mongols attempted a second invasion in 1281 AD, however, a typhoon sank the entire fleet smashing their dream to pieces. To the avid seeker, luck may seem random in who it picks and chooses as it pleases.

Chinese Luck

Ancient China never seems to disappoint historians with its fascinating culture and traditions. Even to this day, many actions that we see as normal in the west are considered taboo on the other side of the globe. It is quite interesting, for example, that after being drenched outside, you wouldn't think twice of leaving your opened umbrella to dry out indoors. The Chinese would have never tried this, as it was considered to be a dose of bad luck to have your umbrella opened indoors.

Strict rules were not just applied to umbrellas, even doors made it to the list. The front of a house had to face south to bring good luck and peace into the home. This is a stark contrast to the ancient Indians who lived by the Vaastu system of building houses, where buying a house facing southwards was considered bad luck. In ancient India, extending a north-facing house in a north-easterly direction was considered to bring good luck. Many cultures do not align when luck is concerned, and these are clear examples.

Some of us can't stay still when a bumblebee finds its way into our living rooms, while swinging your hands frantically through the air, you might hit your target with one swipe and count yourself lucky at not being stung. However, for the Chinese killing a bee indoors is a big NO, unless you wanted to welcome years of bad luck into your home. According to superstition, on Chinese New Year children are told to stay awake as long as possible to ensure their parents lived a long life.

Why numbers?

Humanity has even tied numbers to luck to bring about good fortune. The number 8 has a winning spot in the Chinese good luck books, so it is no wonder Chinese lottery entries seem to be bombarded with 8's. The number 8 is also highly regarded in different religions that marvel at its mystery. The story of

Noah's ark mentions 8 humans including Noah on board who escaped the great flood. In Islam, 8 is the number of angels that carry the throne of Allah (God), there are also 8 gates to Paradise. The Chinese have a group of 8 immortals, each with the ability to transfer power to a tool that can bestow life or destroy evil. Considering these beliefs, the number 8 just might be lucky after all.

From ancient Egypt to the Hellenic Greek culture to Africa and South America, numerology has played an important role in cultures that used numbers as a yardstick throughout most of their lives. The number seven was seen as a mystical number and for the most part symbolises power throughout history. Catholicism has 7 sacraments. Some mystics see humans as having 7 major energy centres which correspond to seven levels of consciousness. The beautiful rainbow appearing after a rainstorm consists of seven colours and let us not forget the seven days of the week.

The famous expression "being on cloud 9" has a good reason for throwing 9 into the bag. Nine is both a wonder and of utmost importance in Norse mythology. The magical tree Yggdrasil supports 9 worlds. It also took Hermod 9 nights to try to free Baldr from Niflheim. Odin himself hung for 9 days and nights from Yggdrasil to be able to unravel the mystery of the runes.

The number 9 also appears in Greek mythology especially in the form of the 9 muses (Kallichore, Helike, Eunike, Thelxinoe, Terpsichore, Euterpe, Eukelade, Día, and Enope) which were the deities responsible for providing inspiration and creativity in individuals, such as artists, who required it. The river Styx in Greek mythology was a mystical river that doubled as a deity and formed the boundary between earth and the underworld. It was said to have encircled the underworld 9 times. The number 9, however, is not exactly warmly accepted in every culture. In Japan, for example, the number 9 is not considered lucky and in medieval Germany, people believed that you could enter Fairyland just by twirling around 9 times.

Numbers are indeed fascinating and form a part of our everyday experience. It gives us a measure of what we see in our environment. Control and measure are often considered to go hand in hand, so when you have measured something, it is easier to control.

Ancient Greeks, Hebrews and Chaldeans practised a form of divination through arithmomancy (the practice of assigning numerical values to a word or phrase, by means of a simplified version of ancient Greek isopsephism or Hebrew/Aramaic gematria, as adapted to the Latin alphabet). It was their way of exploring the power and mysteries of the universe. Letters were assigned numbers, and these were added up in such a way to get a special value. The numbers had special meanings and some numbers could bring more luck than others.

Where luck was concerned, it wasn't just numbers that were considered valuable, but also the days of the week. Monday, which the ancient Greeks called Hemera Selenes meaning "day of the moon", was extremely important in different traditions. The pattern of Monday being named after the moon is also followed in China, Japan, Korea and Norway.

The moon was seen as very powerful as it causes the high and low tides of the ocean. In the astrological sense, the moon is connected to one's emotions and holds one's memory.

Some people even go as far as wearing pearls on a Monday to usher in good luck. Even the idea of starting something new on a Monday, such as a project, is considered lucky and it was predicted that you would finish that task successfully and quickly. Also, the astrological star sign under which someone was born was connected to how luck would play out on a particular day of the week. For example, someone born under the sign Leo would be lucky on a Sunday, and this luck would increase by wearing gold. I will elaborate on luck and the star constellations in a later chapter.

The combination of numbers and days of the week also mattered, for example, Tuesday the 13th is considered to be an unlucky day in Greek and Spanish speaking countries and is even considered unluckier than Friday the 13th. In the Bible, Tuesday was counted as the third day of creation. The French "Mardi Gras", meaning Fat Tuesday or more popularly known as Pancake Day also falls on a Tuesday.

We can't discuss lucky days without mentioning the unlucky dates too. Friday the 13th is that "big elephant in the room" that no one wants to address and just the mere mention of it seems to get people's hairs standing on end. But where does all this superstition stem from? There is no one size that fits all. In Britain, for instance, Friday was Hangman's Day which meant that all people that had been condemned to death would be hanged. Though the days of hanging are far behind in

Britain, there is still an uneasy feeling about Friday lingering in the air.

Even though we have all heard of lucky and unlucky days, it doesn't stop some of us nonchalant people from doing what we like on whatever day of the week we choose. However, the question still remains, "what is the remedy to all this bad luck?" There is no one correct answer to provide the solution to everyone's problems, but "preparation is key" as it is often said, seems to be good advice. When it comes to bad luck you are going to have to be prepared.

The ancients were so careful when it came to getting geared up against any sign of bad energy or bad luck, the two of which pretty much went hand in hand in some cases. A lot of these traditions and practices were passed down from one generation to the next. It is easy to navigate this world with careful observation of what is around us, but would you feel a bit uneasy if all eyes were on you? You might whip your mirror out of your pocket and wonder what all the fuss is about only to find out that you are looking decent after all. Eyes were a big thing back in the day and still is to this day.

The symbol of the eye can be seen on many monumental buildings including cathedrals with many people walking by carelessly unaware of the eye's real meaning. This quasi-universal symbol of protection against evil is very prominent in the Mediterranean and North African traditions, as well as other parts of the world. In these places, "the evil eye" as it is often called is a look or stare that brings about bad luck in someone's life. In these cultures, someone's envy or dislike caused them to keep their eye on you and render you useless through the instrument of the evil eye. This is the reason why the blue evil eye was worn as a talisman to protect the person from evil spirits and bad luck. The earliest ever recorded Evil Eye is believed to have been discovered in Northern Syria and Iraq on Mesopotamian clay tablets over 5000 years ago and may actually have originated as early as the Upper Palaeolithic age. On a personal note, being born and raised in the Mediterranean culture, I believe the real evil eye is just negative energy radiating from a jealous or envious soul. Our bodies emit energy and you can feel when someone really wishes you good fortune, or alternatively, you may feel uncomfortable in the presence of someone emitting negative energy.

In ancient Egyptian mythology, the symbol of the eye represents the eye of Horus, the god whose one eye was the moon and the other was the sun. After fighting and defeating his enemy Seth, Horus became the King of Life and as a result, his evil eyes were believed to have the ultimate power because of the curse they could inflict. In Ancient Greece, the intriguing concept of the evil eye dates back to the 6th century B.C. where it was commonly shown on drinking vessels. Great minds like Plato and Plutarch have tried to explain its function, where the latter emphasised that the eyes were the source of deadly rays emanating from the inner recesses of the evil eye. Such an evil glare is given when one least expects it.

To guard against this, talismans or amulets were moulded into the shape of an eye. Blue and green were the traditional colours used in its design, which both increased spiritual protection. In today's world, repellents may be used to drive away annoying mosquitos, but the evil eye acted as a repellent against evil forces and bad luck. These talismans come in different shapes and were often worn as bracelets or pendants. They could be found hanging over the main door or the entrance to someone's home. As people would often act on instinct, talismans were used when added protection was needed. So, the next time you are at a store or restaurant and you see the evil eye swinging above your head, just remember - it's for your own good.

In ancient times, especially in India, people used to light incense sticks outside their homes to keep bad luck and evil spirits away. People also used to write certain words and curses on their walls to repel bad luck. Today, in many Asian countries, it is believed that burning raw red chillies in a fire makes bad luck go away. In countries like India and Pakistan, it is staunchly believed that if you had a bad experience, touching the chillies and then burning them in a fire makes the bad luck go away forever.

Animals and plants also have their place in the world of luck. In Thailand, the elephant is considered to be good luck regardless of the direction its trunk is facing. In Ancient Persia, Huma was a mystical bird of fortune and good luck that lived in Paradise itself, a legendary creature from the Sufi fables. It is believed to never land and lives its entire life airborne. It flies invisibly high above the earth, almost impossible to spot with the human eye. Also referred to as the bird of fortune, the Huma bird is a compassionate creature and symbolizes happiness.

According to the Sufi lore, once you catch a glimpse of Huma or even its shadow, happiness will ensue for the rest of your life. The prominent Sufi preacher Inayat Khan portrays the spiritual dimension of this bird. According to him, it represents the evolution of thought to the zenith where it breaks all limitations. "Huma" in the Persian language stands for the fabulous bird. It was believed that if this legendary creature sat on the head of an individual, then it was an omen to that person becoming a king. In the word Huma, "hu" represents the spirit and the word "ma" is Arabic meaning "water". In older traditions, it was believed that the Zoroaster, the founder of the ancient Persian religion, was born of the Huma tree.

In ancient Babylon [3], a variety of feasts were celebrated, most notably during the month of Elul (September). In Elul, we find that every day is dedicated to a god, and certain rites and ceremonies were prescribed for each. The first day is dedicated to Anu and Bel, a day of good luck. When during the month of Elul the moon was seen, the shepherd of mighty nations would offer to the moon, as a free-will offering, a gazelle without blemish. He would make his free-will offering to the Sun (the mistress of the world) and to the Moon (the supreme god) while lifting up his hand finds to find favour with the god.

The second day was dedicated to the goddesses. The king made his free-will offering once again to the Sun and the Moon while lifting up his hands.

The 3rd day is a fast day dedicated to Merodach and Zarpanit. *A lucky day*. During the night in the presence of Merodach and Istar, the king makes his free-will offering. He offers sacrifices. The lifting up of his hand finds favour with the god.

The 4th day is the feast-day of Nebo (the son of Merodach). *A lucky day.* During the night, in the presence of Nebo and Tasmit, the king makes his freewill offering. He offers sacrifices. The lifting up of his hand he presents to the god.

The 5th day is dedicated to the Lord of the lower firmament and the Lady of the lower firmament. *A lucky day.* During the night, in the presence of Assur and Nin-lil, the king makes his free-will offering. He offers sacrifices. The lifting up of his hand finds favour with the god.

The 6th day is dedicated to Rimmon and Nin-lil. *A lucky day.* The king repeats a penitential psalm and a litany. During the night, before the east wind, the king makes his free-will offering to Rimmon. He offers sacrifices. The lifting up of his hand he presents to the god.

The 7th day is a fast-day, dedicated to Merodach and Zarpanit. *A lucky day.* A day of rest (Sabbath). The shepherd of mighty nations must not eat flesh cooked at the fire or in the smoke. His clothes he must not change. White garments he must not put on. He must not offer sacrifice. The king must not drive a chariot. He must not issue royal decrees. In a secret place the augur must not mutter. Medicine for the sickness of his body he must not apply. For making a curse it is not fit. During the night the king makes his free-will offering before Merodach and

Istar. He offers sacrifice. The lifting up of his hand finds favour with the god.

The 8th day is the feast of Nebo. *A lucky day.* During the night the shepherd of mighty nations directs his hand to the sacrifice of a sheep.

The 9th day is dedicated to Adar and Gula. *A lucky day.* During the night, in the presence of Adar and Gula, the king makes his free-will offering. He offers sacrifice. The lifting up of his hand he presents to the god.

The 10th day is dedicated to the mistress of the lower firmament and the divine Judge. *A lucky day.* During the night, in the presence of the star of the chariot and the star of the son of Istar, the king makes his free-will offering. He offers sacrifice. The lifting up of his hand finds favour with the god.

The 11th day is the completion of the meal-offering to Tasmit and Zarpanit. *A lucky day.* When the moon lifts up its crown of moonlight, and its orb rejoices, the king makes his free-will offering to the moon. He offers sacrifice. The lifting up of his hand finds favour with the god.

The 12th day is the gift-day of Bel and Beltis. *A lucky day.* The king makes his free-will offering to Bel and Beltis. He offers sacrifices. The lifting up of his hand finds favour with the god.

The 13th day is sacred to the Moon the supreme god. *A lucky day.* The moon lifts up its crown of moonlight towards the earth. On this day assuredly the king makes his free-will offering to the Sun-god the mistress of the world, and the Moon the supreme god. He offers sacrifice. The lifting up of his hand finds favour with the god.

The 14th day is sacred to Beltis and Nergal. *A lucky day*. A Sabbath. The shepherd of mighty nations must not eat flesh cooked on the fire or in the smoke. The clothing of his body he must not change. White garments he must not put on. He must not offer sacrifice. He must not drive a chariot. He must not issue royal decrees. In a secret place the augur must not mutter. Medicine for the sickness of his body he must not apply. For making a curse it is not fit. In the night the king makes his free-will offering to Beltis and Nergal. He offers sacrifice.

The 15th day is sacred to the Sun the Lady of the House of Heaven. A day for making the stated offering to Sin the supreme god. *A lucky day*. The king makes his free-will offering to Samas the mistress of the world, and Sin the supreme god. He offers sacrifice.

The 16th day is a fast-day to Merodach and Zarpanit. *A lucky day*. The king must not repeat a penitential psalm. In the night, before Merodach and Istar, the king presents his free-will offering. He offers sacrifice.

The 17th day is the feast-day of Nebo and Tasmit. *A lucky day*. In the night, before Nebo and Tasmit, the king presents his free-will offering He offers sacrifice. The lifting up of his hands finds favour with the god.

The 18th day is the festival of Sin and Samas. *A lucky day.* The king presents his free-will offering to Samas the mistress of the world, and Sin the supreme god. He offers sacrifice.

As we can see here even the mightiest of kings in Babylon prayed for and begged the gods for Luck, which might be given in the form of a blessing ray of energy granted only by heaven.

"If a man be lucky, there is no telling the possible extent of his good fortune. Pitch him into the Euphrates and he will swim out with a pearl in his hand." - Babylonian Proverb

Royal Luck

Throughout the centuries, the fascination with luck and good fortune was not exclusive to the public. Kings, Queens, Sultans, Emperors and Caliphs have consulted their own designated royal court astrologers for nearly everything, from the time of having the first meal of the day to when a battle should be waged to whom the crown prince shall marry.

Those mystical astrologers worked as physicians also, since astrology was connected to health and well-being.

One of the most famous royal astrologers in the middle ages was a man named Albumasar (Abū Maʻshar Jaʻfar Al-Balkhi), who was born on August 787 and died in March 886 AD.

He was an early Persian[4] Muslim astrologer, thought to be the greatest astrologer of the Abbasid court in Baghdad. While he was not a major innovator, his practical manuals for training astrologers profoundly influenced Muslim intellectual history and, through translations, that of Western Europe and Byzantium. In his famous book, Introduction to Astrology, he said "by observing the great variations of movements in the planets and the stars above, we can understand the possible changes in our world".

As early as Roman Britain, the Druids were described as learned in astrology. Written evidence exists of Druids predicting a child's future from its birthdate. Then we have Alfred the great who went out of his way to translate an astrological text by the Roman philosopher Boethius and applied it to his rule. Whilst later in the 8th century apparently a York-educated astrologer Alcuin, served as a close advisor to Emperor Charlemagne. With the Norman conquest came a whole new wave of astrological texts through William the Conqueror's court which contained work from Jewish scholars, bringing with them astrological Intel from Arabic, Moorish and Jewish sources. With quite an impact on the status quo, William the Conqueror himself used his astrologer to set the date of his coronation, the auspicious hour of midnight, Xmas day 1066.[5]

Indeed, since the first days of civilization, people sought refuge and assurances through consulting the stars and the planets. They saw them as gods to be worshipped and built high rising monuments to be closer to heaven and the gods. The effect of the massive infinite dome above us on our luck, fortune and future still dominate our thinking in the modern day.

Chapter 2

Ovarian Lottery, Luck And The Myth Of Hard Work

Ovarian Lottery, Luck And The Myth Of Hard Work

Sometimes life is like the Lotto, where only a select few are fortunate enough to walk away with the Jackpot and the rest go home with nothing. We are all born equal in a way – we come into this world naked and helpless, but as time goes by some get a golden spoon with heaps of fortune, luck and success and the supply never runs dry. It is as if some invisible magical force follows them and makes them successful. These giants are so fortunate, their legacy lives on after they pass.

So, what is the secret? Is luck the secret ingredient or is it just destiny or perhaps (as we were told all along), it is all about hard work?

In this chapter, I am challenging the outdated notion that hard work is the only way to success. It is not. I will be presenting you with real-life stories and events that prove beyond any reasonable doubt, that luck and destiny are major players in our life and success.

Success is largely a lucky event

Successful people, who believe they do it all on their own, are almost certainly wrong. To be successful, every one in a long list of events must happen.

Professor Daniel Kahneman (an emeritus professor of psychology and public affairs at Princeton University) who won the 2002 Nobel Prize in Economics states that the difference between moderate and great success is mostly luck, not skill.

Chance plays a much greater role in our lives than we might wish or realize.

Nassim Taleb who is a well-known author, mathematical statistician and risk analyst argues that $1 million earned as a dentist is not the same as $1 million earned as a rockstar because success as an artist depends much more on chance. If you imagine a game of "career roulette," you end up a starving artist 99 times for every time you end up a rockstar. If you want to minimize the chance of bad luck, he says, be a dentist. There are no "starving dentists" [1]

Most people will never know what it is like to be successful. When we grow up, our parents do not teach us to be successful, they tell us to work hard. Everything was hard after that. It was hard to fit in at school, studying was hard, exams were even harder and to be top of your class was reserved for the golden pupils. We all knew a golden child in school– the one that sailed through everything, got a first in matric, rushed through a few degrees on route to the predestined golden corporate ladder that they climbed like a professional trapeze artist to the top – securing the revered CEO seat in record time. It was as if luck followed them, embraced them, and crowned them king or queen of success and gave them a corner office with a view and a luxury company car.

We envy those who have success bestowed on them and we often try to find a flaw in their magical pathway to success, but even that eludes us. We ask ourselves, "how did they do it and why can I not be successful too?"

Experts provide us with a long list of elements – 'ingredients' for success and this list usually includes – amongst various other buzzwords: accept challenges, set goals, be ready to work hard, give it your all, learn and never stop learning, be focused and determined and never give up. The catchwords are not provided with instructions on how to apply them – like a recipe to bake a cake. If only we knew what to mix, what to cook with butter and what to grind – then we could whip up a perfect recipe for success. We usually take the buzzwords we are comfortable with and we whip them into something hoping for success.

Unlike the perfect cake recipe, there is no perfect recipe for success. Thus our 'baking' sometimes fails and we lose interest – we give up on being successful and we settle for second-best. Some people even settle for mediocrity, as it is easier when no one expects much from you – then you cannot fail.

Many keep on trying to reach success and end up feeling frustrated all the time. It is difficult when you are in the game and you are forever missing the goalpost, and you never win.

I have seen many employees settle for being average just to get a pay check at the end of the month. They don't work any harder than they need to, and they are happy with that. They find achievement, satisfaction, and success in something else: a second job, a hobby or sport. For many, an office is just a place that pays the rent. Sometimes an average Joe gets lucky and they get promoted to the corner office with the nice view. The sudden promotion does not come with a guarantee for success and if average Joe is not equipped to face the challenge, he fails again.

Most of us have tried and failed even though we were determined, we learned, worked hard and persevered. It felt like success was an elusive factor that we just could not reach or hold onto it. Is success just a lucky break reserved for a chosen few?

Not all CEOs are successful either and they sadly often take the whole company down with them when they fail. So, the question begs, why can't we all be successful? What is holding us back?

I hope to unravel the mystery of being successful, with all the buzzwords and ever-elusive luck. Perhaps we can all be successful if we get to the 'bottom of it'. I certainly would like to know the secret to ultimate success myself.

The Ovarian Lottery

In 1997, Warren Buffett, the famous investor and multi-billionaire, proposed a thought experiment. "Imagine that it is 24 hours before you are going to be born," he said, "and a genie comes to you."

"The genie says you can design the rules of the society you are about to enter. You get to design the social, economic, and governmental rules, and those rules will prevail for your lifetime and your children's lifetime and your grandchildren's lifetime."

"But there is a catch," he said.

"You don't know whether you're going to be born rich or poor, male or female, infirm or able-bodied, in the United States or Afghanistan. All you know is that you get to take one ball out of a barrel with 5.8 billion (1997 world population) balls in it - and that's you."

"In other words," Buffett continues, "you're going to participate in what I call the Ovarian Lottery, and that is the most important thing that's ever going to happen to you in your life. It's going to determine way more than what school you go to, how hard you work, it will determine all kinds of things." Buffett has long been a proponent for the role of luck in success. In his 2014 Annual Letter, he wrote, "Through dumb luck, [my business partner] Charlie and I were born in the United States, and we are forever grateful for the staggering advantages this accident of birth has given us."

When explained in this way, it seems hard to deny the importance of luck, randomness, and good fortune in life. Indeed, these factors play a critical role.

As a general rule, the wilder the success, the more extreme and unlikely the circumstances that caused it. It's often a combination of the right genes, the right connections, the right timing, and a thousand other influences that nobody is wise enough to predict.[2]

Give me luck and throw me in the ocean

In his book 'Outliers. The Story of Success' Canadian journalist Malcolm Gladwell sought to identify why extraordinarily successful individuals are so successful. His central hypothesis is that personality traits, intelligence, etc., are of minor importance in explaining the success of exceptional individuals and he attributes a large proportion of the success of people like Bill Gates and Steve Jobs to a chain of happy coincidences.

If a successful person had not happened to be at a specific place at just the right time or had not known the right people, they would never have become successful. The reader is constantly confronted with questions such as: What would have happened if Bill Gates hadn't had the opportunity to work on a large computer for free? Would Gates still have achieved such incredible success in his field? It is difficult to pursue such assumptions to any kind of satisfactory conclusion. If this single event or that one stroke of luck hadn't happened, what would have been different?[3]

Virtually every career path constitutes what the cognitive psychologists Amos Tversky and Daniel Kahneman have called a conjunctive process. To succeed, each of a long sequence of events must occur. "Even when each of these events is very likely," they wrote, "the overall probability of success can be quite low if the number of events is large." Tversky and Kahneman demonstrated the existence of a widespread tendency for people to overestimate the likelihood of success of conjunctive processes.[4]

When we see a successful result, we incline to think that it must have been inevitable. In reality, each of the numerous steps along a typical career path depends on all the ones preceding it. Even small changes early in the course can once dramatically change the result.

Luck as Fate's Executioner

I believe luck and destiny go hand in hand, you can't separate the two. If you are destined to live a happy healthy and wealthy life then you are destined to be lucky by default.

We are accountable for how we choose to respond to life's events and for how rigorously we prepare ourselves to receive fate's executioner, Luck.

We need to be ready psychologically, spiritually, intellectually, and physiologically, amid the apparent absence of luck, for luck's inevitable arrival or return. This inner 'psychological preparedness' might mean the difference between good and bad fortune. Without such inner preparation and readiness, we may fail to recognize or reply to this transitory yet fateful moment in our lives, permitting luck to uneventfully and unfortunately pass us by.

Luck is an existential potentiality that life presents to us, good or bad. The key is to be patient, observant, self-aware, and psychologically ready to recognize that potentiality when and if it arises, and then to be able and willing to respond or act truthfully in that time. Knowing when to wait, when to listen introspectively, when to feel, when to contemplate, and when to act fearlessly are all crucial. Although all of this seems like a powerless existence, we do have a limited amount of power and freedom to cause or prevent anything from happening. Waiting for luck does not mean we should sit and surrender, far from it, it means to be ready no matter what is thrown at us.

Vincent van Gogh

Vincent van Gogh struggled through his whole life to find success and he only sold one painting during his lifetime. The Red Vineyard sold for 400 francs in Belgium seven months before his death. His most expensive painting, the Portrait of Dr Gachet was sold for $148.6 million in 1990. Today his paintings are unaffordable and they are hanging in museums all over the world. Was he denied luck when he was alive? What is the benefit to all this fame when he is no longer alive and enjoying the fruits of his work?

Violet Jessop

Violet Jessop was a nurse and ocean liner stewardess who earned the nickname "Miss Unsinkable" by surviving both the accidents of the Titanic in 1912 and its sister ship, the HMHS Britannic, which met the same fate in 1916. Jessup was also reportedly on board a third boat, the RMS Olympic when it hit a warship - but fortunately, the Olympic stayed afloat.[5]

Maarten de Jonge

In 2014, there were two tragic plane crashes involving Malaysian Air flights. The first was shot down over Ukraine, and the second disappeared without a trace somewhere over the Indian Ocean in the greatest aviation mystery of all time. Beyond the fact that both incidents involved the same airline in such a short period, there was another striking coincidence:

Dutch cyclist Maarten de Jonge was scheduled to take both flights, but cheated death by bumping his ticket at the eleventh hour when cheaper options became available.[6]

Tsutomo Yamaguchi

Tsutomo Yamaguchi is either incredibly lucky or incredibly unlucky, depending on how you look at it. He is unlucky in that he happened to be in both Hiroshima and Nagasaki at the time of their catastrophic atomic bombings, and yet lucky that he miraculously survived both. Yamaguchi reportedly fled Hiroshima in search of safety, winding up in Nagasaki only to see the second flash of white light that would cover over half of his body in burns from radioactive ash. Yamaguchi is the only person recognized by the Japanese government as having survived both bombings.[7]

Stephen Hawking

Stephen Hawking shares his birth and death dates with Galileo and Einstein, respectively.

The theoretical physicist, cosmologist, and author was famously born on the 300th anniversary of Galileo's death and died on what would have been Einstein's 139th birthday. That said, the far more confounding question of statistical improbability surrounding Hawking's life was the fact that he survived to be 76 despite living with Lou Gehrig's Disease. Though we know very little about the disease, according to Scientific American, most of those diagnosed live for about five years past diagnosis. Hawking survived for more than five additional decades, allowing him to share his crucial insights and gifts with the world—not to mention his legendary humour.[8]

Joseph Figlock

In Detroit sometime in the 1930s, a young (if incredibly careless) mother must have been eternally grateful to a man named Joseph Figlock. As Figlock was walking down the street, the mother's baby fell from a high window onto Figlock. The baby's fall was broken, and both Figlock and the baby were unharmed. A stroke of luck on its own, but a year later, the very same baby fell from the very same window onto poor, unsuspecting Joseph Figlock as he was again passing beneath, and again, they both survived the event.[9]

Even in Football, Luck is the winner

Luck is also a major factor in sport. The athletes in this year's Olympic Games (2021) will have to perform without spectator support, something very important to performance.

In Chris Anderson and David Sally's book 'The Numbers Game', football comes down to 50 per cent skill and 50 per cent luck. Anderson, an economics and politics professor at Warwick University in the UK, said "football is driven more by luck and chance than any other team sport". "There's the 50 per cent that can be controlled, like tactics, team selection and preparation. The other half is all chance."[10]

When teams are mismatched, luck will never be enough to compensate for the lower-rated team. Without skilled players,

managers and tactics, luck is of little value in itself. On th
hand, when the teams are equally matched, luck can be a
decisive factor. When the teams are equal, a 1%-3% chance can
mean the difference between winning and losing. On the one
hand, it highlights the importance of preparation, on the other,
the importance of luck!

The probability of luck can be estimated, but its impact
cannot be quantified. When luck does not matter, it's worthless.
When it does, it's priceless.[11]

The famous Spanish footballer Gerard Piqué who plays as
a centre-back for the Spanish club Barcelona once said: 'When
you're in the semi-finals of the Champions League, you need to
be really good and need a little bit of luck.'

Marcelo, a Brazilian footballer who plays for the Spanish
club Real Madrid once described the penalties as like the
lottery: ''Penalties are like the lottery and you miss them when
luck is not on your side.''

Hard work is just a Myth

We all want to believe that hard work leads to something
good: a promotion, a pay rise, some sort of recognition. It is an
idea that is repeated often by those who have seen (especially
financial) success. President Donald Trump famously bragged:
"Hard work is my personal method for financial success." In
2019 he tweeted: "No president ever worked harder than me!"
Which should probably be our first clue that the idea is deeply
flawed.[12]

When we tell everyone else that success simply comes down to hard work, we are setting them up for a nasty psychological cycle of failure. They will work hard and when they don't get noticed, they will tell themselves, it is their fault. So, they work even harder, and the cycle continues, until they reach burnout.[13]

What about the idea that success is due mainly to personal qualities such as talent, intelligence, skills, smarts, efforts, hard work or risk-taking? If success could be purely attributed to our IQ, then the most talented people would be the most successful. The average IQ in the UK is 100 and only one-third of people have a score above 115, with the top 1% reaching a score of 135 or above. However, if you think about it, the variances are still relatively small - nobody has an IQ of 1,000!

Hard work is a similar scenario. The average actual hours worked in the UK has remained steady for decades, around 38h per week. Perhaps you work hard and put in 60 or even 70 hours per week, but anything more than that is not sustainable over a long period and nobody can work 1,000 hours a week. We all only have 24 hours in a day.

If the difference in material success cannot be explained with intellect and talent, or hours worked, where does success come from? The Italian physicists Alessandro Pluchino and Andrea Raspisarda teamed up with the Italian economist Alessio Biondo to conduct the first-ever experiment to quantify the role of luck and talent in successful jobs. They used a computer simulation of success defined by financial wealth to show that the most successful people in the world necessarily the most talented. They are the luckiest.

They found out that luck plays a much greater role than most people realize.

"We discovered a strict correlation between luck and success. Encountering a series of lucky events was responsible for incredible success even if individual talent was lower than super talented people. This is what we usually see around us in the real world. There are plenty of instances of people who we don't consider particularly smart but in some way they reach a high level of wealth and success."

Of course, you need a certain level of talent to be able to exploit lucky opportunities. The researchers say that this "talent" can be anything from the capacity for hard work to intelligence, to being hard-working, but talent alone is not enough. In the simulation, the most talented people only made up a small portion of the successful people.[14]

A lot of successful people don't work hard, they work smart. I believe the reason for that is their momentum. They sustained good habits thus gaining that powerful momentum that reduces the requirement for hard work. Like a rocket shooting into space, it uses the most fuel during the take-off phase but once it's outside the earth's crippling gravity, it can glide with minimal fuel.

Charlie Munger: Fish where the fish are

Charlie Munger has a great analogy for working on the right project. He tells us to fish where the fish are. There is no point in dragging yourself up at 5 a.m. in the cold darkness, diligently prepping your fishing gear, heading out on the water only to sit around for 3 hours in an area without a single fish! That's a waste of hard work.

Here is Munger explaining this to Berkshire Hathaway shareholders:

"The first rule of fishing is - fish where the fish are, and the second rule of fishing is don't forget rule number one. In investing it is the same thing. Some places have lots of fish, and you don't have to be that good a fisherman to do pretty well. Other places are so heavily fished that no matter how good a fisherman you are, you aren't going to do very well.[15]

The question remains, don't you need to be lucky to be in a fishy place?

Chapter 3

Luck And Religion

Luck And Religion

Throughout history, the world's major religions have long held serious convictions on the subject of luck. In the Islam holy book, the Quran, the word luck appears in a couple of different verses. One refers to Qaroun (Korah), one of the richest men in the old world, where the holy verse describes him as being of 'great luck'.

Buddhists, meanwhile, have mixed views on luck. Zen Buddhists do not believe there is any transcendent power of good fortune. Zen Buddhists believe all things are caused by something, particularly karma. In general, however, many of the world's 500 million Buddhists continue to offer fruit to ancestors for luck or to wear good luck amulets.

In Hinduism, the predominant religion of India, adherents often pray for the blessings of Lakshmi, the goddess of luck and success. During Diwali, the festival of lights, many Hindus draw rangoli (folk art) on floors to lure luck .[1]

Most Christians do not believe in luck, but rather that the will of God controls our lives, while in Judaism, there is a special holy lottery called The Gra lottery! Many Jewish schools of thought believe in luck as God's tool.

Let us here explore this intriguing connection between religion and luck.

Luck in Zoroastrianism

Zoroastrianism is one of the world's oldest continuously practised religions. Originating in ancient Persia, it was founded in the 5th century BC by a prophet and religious reformer named Zarathustra, also known as Zoroaster in Greek. Zoroastrians believe in one God (Ahura Mazda), and that one day the forces of good will defeat the forces of evil and restore the world to its original state of perfection.

Zoroastrians have a concept called Khvarenah, it is an Avestan word for a Zoroastrian idea literally meaning "glory" or "splendour" but understood as a divine mystical force or power projected upon and aiding the appointed. The neuter noun thus also connotes "divine royal glory", reflecting the perceived divine empowerment of kings. The term also carries a secondary meaning of "good luck and fortune"; with those who possess it being able to complete their mission or function. Bisyllabic Khvarenah is only attested once in the Gathas, the oldest hymns of Zoroastrianism, and considered to have been composed by the Prophet himself. The one instance of Gathic Khvarenah occurs in Yasna 51.18, where the word appears to mean royal glory. The primary source of information on Khvarenah comes from the Yashts, the younger Avesta's collection of 21 hymns dedicated to individual divinities.

In the 9th-12th century AD texts of Zoroastrian tradition, Khvarenah is a spiritual force that exists before the creation of the mortal body. In these later texts, the glory appears to be acquirable through learning and knowledge. Khvarenah continues to be identified with astral bodies, but its primary function is in its role as the divine glory of kings, the continuation of the Avestan notion of the Kavam Khvarenah.

The identification of Khvarenah with religion is a new concept. The Kar-namag i Ardashir, a collection of hagiographic legends related to Ardashir the founder of the Sassanid Empire, includes a tale in which Ardashir – who at that point in the story is still a vassal of the Arsacid Parthians – escapes from the court of the last Arsacid king, Ardavan. In the story, Ardashir makes off with much of Ardavan's treasure, as well as Ardavan's favourite beautiful concubine, and is being chased by Ardavan and his troops. On the road, Ardavan and his contingent are overtaken by an enormous ram, which is also following Ardashir. Ardavan's religious advisors explain that the ram is the manifestation of the Khvarenah of the ancient Iranian kings, which is leaving Ardavan and the Parthians in favour of a new emperor.

The representation of Khvarenah as a ram reappears on Sassanid seals and as an ornament in Sassanid architecture. It also appears in Sassanian crowns as a bird with a pearl in its beak.[2]

Luck in Judaism

Judaism is an Abrahamic ethnic religion comprising the collective religious, cultural, and legal traditions and civilization of the Jewish people. Judaism is considered by religious Jews to be the expression of the covenant that God established with the Children of Israel. It encompasses a wide body of texts, practices, theological positions, and forms of organization. The Torah is part of the larger text known as the Tanakh or the Hebrew Bible, and supplemental oral tradition represented by later texts such as the Midrash and the Talmud. With between 14.5 and 17.4 million adherents worldwide, Judaism is the tenth-largest religion in the world.[3]

Let us explore how Judaism views luck? The Torah cautions "you shall not believe in lucky times" (Leviticus 19:26). The idea that an object can bring luck is completely foreign to Judaism as the idea is that God runs the world and that it is up to us to make the most of the opportunities, we have to fulfil our unique goals, is central to Judaism. Prayer and Jewish rituals are tools to help us achieve our goals, not because they contain any magical powers, but because they help train us to access and appreciate the spiritual world.[4]

The Bible is very clear that luck has no impact on our lives, ''There is no magic in Jacob and no divination in Israel" (Numbers 23:23).

Rabbi Jeremy Rosen who is an Orthodox rabbi, author, and lecturer wrote that in Judaism, astrology's link with mysticism gave it continued relevance and influence so that today there are many "rabbis" who use astrology and its allied systems to help the sick and the disturbed try to cope with the pressures of life. Snake oil salesmen, hustlers, and 'Ponzis' still make a good living. There is a major divide in Judaism between rationalists and non-rationalists. On this point, Rabbi Rosen sides with the rationalists. Evil spirits, bad luck, and the evil eye are only relevant to people who are credulous, uneducated, or desperate enough to believe in them. Humans who face an insurmountable crisis turn wherever they can for sustenance and support, and Judaism must offer them that. As they used to say in World War I, "There are no atheists in trenches." He does not want to equate turning to God in despair or from the depths, which is a profound human expression, with belief in magic or luck.

It is true there are areas in our lives that we have control over and areas where we do not. But if you do not study hard, you are unlikely to pass an exam. If you do not apply for a job, you are likely to remain unemployed. If you do not make an effort to meet the sort of partner you want to marry, you are more likely to get involved with someone unsuitable. There are other areas where events beyond our control cause things to happen to us. Is the act of getting on a plane that then crashes a matter of bad luck, or is it the absence of information about a bomb or fault in the engine that results in death? Insurance companies rely on statistics, on probability for a good reason.

Statistics and probability are not a certainty, but it works better than anything else in predicting things. Investment advice based on hunches may work occasionally, but over time the cold numbers tell a more reliable story. There are general trends and specific exceptions in everything, including life expectancy, susceptibility to disease, and everything else in life. Is it bad luck to catch a virus or a disease? Bacteria are part of our world. Who is to blame if one affects you badly? We all take risks all the time. Whenever we get into a car, we know that a certain percentage of travellers will be killed on the roads. We just hope the drunken driver coming the other way misses us or stayed behind for another drink. We go about our lives knowing we will all die one day. Is it luck if I die at 40, 70, or 90? Is it luck that decides who will be president, or make a fortune?

We make use of the circumstances of our time. Rockefeller made money out of oil, Bill Gates made it on computers and Zuckerberg on the internet. Similarly, we suffer from the negative circumstances of our time, be they war or peace. If we keep fit, we will more likely resist disease. If we keep spiritually alive, we will better survive trials and tests. But there is no magic, no luck that will protect us from the realities and challenges of life. Charms, promises, and holy water are placebos. Placebos work because people want them to but they have nothing to do with luck. Rabbi Rosen emphasis that faith helps us cope. There is, however, a difference between having faith in God to help us cope and believing that whether God acts good or bad depends on hocus pocus. It is goodness that appeals to the Almighty, not charms. What we should mean by luck comes from reducing the odds and taking advantage of situations wherever they may happen. The luck that we make is far more effective than the luck others promise us.[5]

Lottery & Luck as an act of God!

In his mind-blowing research paper titled: 'Using Lotteries in Logic of Halakhah Law, The Meaning of Randomness in Judaism', Professor Ely Merzbach who is a renowned Jewish mathematician and emeritus professor at Bar-Ilan University's Department of Mathematics, argues that there are many phenomena in the Bible connected to the idea of the random, generally in a positive light, but sometimes in a negative one. Both in the Talmudic literature and in the Halakhah texts, the hazal (the Sages) also relate to random processes. As we will see here, for them every chance event has a clear meaning, usually even a holy one. In fact, every culture in the world relates to randomness. However, from the Greek philosophers until the rationalism of the 19th century, a process of denuding randomness of its holiness has been taking place. In Judaism, a lottery is not a blind process; moreover, the randomness has a clear and profound theological meaning.

To this day, there is no precise definition of randomness. A random event is thought to be something that happens with no meaning and no clear cause. In the modern world, the holiness of the random is completely absent. There is a branch of mathematics called Probability Theory, which deals with the quantitative aspects of randomness, developing axioms, and investigating concepts such as independent (unconditional) events, stochastic processes, and borderline occurrences. Despite the success of Probability Theory, not a word has been said about the deeper meaning of the accidental. Computer scientists try to develop algorithms, which are able to produce pseudo-random numbers, but the creative powers of man are incapable of creating true randomness. Apparently, the creation of randomness demands a higher level of complexity than what is actually known to man. The special relationship of hazal to randomness is not confined merely to the realms of philosophy and thought, but also carries with it fundamental implications for the way man lives his daily life. This can be seen in many laws regarding lotteries. It would appear that due to Judaism's absorption of western culture over tens of generations, these laws are not frequently encountered today.

Today we are used to thinking that we, the human race, are subject to not only chance or fate but that we ourselves actually create our own fate. This does not mean that we have no control over our own lives. We always have free choice to do what we wish. This outlook means to say that the existentialist view of freedom sees our lives as having a certain direction or chosen tendency. Looking backwards, a person does not see his own life as wholly random.

The importance of the meaning of randomness appears in both philosophy and deed. In Judaism, there is a deep connection between thought and deed, and they cannot be disconnected one from the other.[6]

Luck and the Jewish Gra Lottery!

What is the Gra lottery? It is the random opening of a sacred book (either once or seven times, depending on the tradition one follows), usually the entire Hebrew Bible, the Pentateuch or the Book of Psalms, reading the first verse that comes up, and deciding on the correct answer based on the verse. Although the practice was attributed to Rabbi Eliyahu ben Shlomo Zalman, the legendary 18th-century scholar known as the Vilna Gaon or the Gra, during the 19th and 20th centuries, in fact, it is mentioned in sources long before his time. Not everyone permits themselves to participate in the Gra lottery, and usually, it was held by someone of high religious status, with the ability to interpret the answer concealed in the text.

Participating in the Gra lottery is also accompanied by fasting, prayer and charity and its results are considered a conclusive answer.

The Gra lottery is only one (and certainly not the most significant) of the lotteries used by Jews throughout history, either to make a ruling or to divine the unknown. The Bible mentions several very significant uses of lotteries: The series of rituals performed by the High Priest on Yom Kippur in the Temple is accompanied by a lottery: "And Aaron shall cast lots upon the two goats: one lot for the Lord, and the other lot for Azazel" (Leviticus 16: 8). The process of the division of inheritances of the tribes in the Land of Israel is based on a lottery: "According to the lot shall their inheritance be divided" (Numbers 26: 56). A lottery was involved in the affair of the avenging of the rape of the concubine in Gibeah (Judges 20), and in the distribution of jobs in the Temple by David (I Chronicles 25: 8), to name but a few.[7]

Serious Question

Professor Ely Merzbach who I quoted above was asked whether it is worth it to buy and play the lottery? His answer was: ''Mathematically speaking, the answer is negative. '' His answer made me wonder, under which law (if any) do the lottery winners get decided?

Luck in Christianity

Most Christians believe there is no such thing as luck, and everything is in the hands of God. The Bible presents a God who is absolutely sovereign over all of the affairs of the world (Ps. 115.3). He is in complete control and he has ordained all things that come to pass. There is absolutely nothing that escapes his notice. He is not only sovereign over your salvation (Eph. 1) but he is also a sovereign bird feeder (Matt. 6.26). He is sovereign over the weather, whether 'good' or 'bad' (Matt. 5.45; Job 38) and He is sovereign over the outcome of a roll of the dice (Prov. 16.33). There is nothing that comes to pass by chance, but rather all things come to pass through the sovereign providence of God.[8]

Charles Spurgeon (19 June 1834 – 31 January 1892) who was an English Baptist preacher wrote: "I believe that every particle of dust that dances in the sunbeam does not move an atom more or less than God wishes – that every particle of spray that dashes against the steamboat has its orbit, as well as the sun in the heavens – that the chaff from the hand of the winnower is steered as the stars in their courses. The creeping of an aphid over the rosebud is as much fixed as the march of the devastating pestilence – the fall of leaves from a poplar is as fully ordained as the tumbling of an avalanche."

It is Not Good Luck — It is a Good God!

Luck has two somewhat contradictory meanings. The original term is related to destiny as pre-determined by a deity or force—what we might call providence. Eastern religions in particular believe luck can be somewhat controlled by superstitious actions. Religious rites are performed (like rubbing the stomach of a Buddha statue or lighting incense) to induce supernatural powers to change the fortune of an adherent. Today, luck more often refers to an event that is out of the control of those involved and has significant repercussions, whether good or bad. This type of luck is related to the chaos theory which points out that most situations are affected by so many elements, that the outcome appears random and certainly unpredictable. The Bible rejects the second type of luck and is cautious with the first. God cannot be manipulated to endow good fortune through superstitious practices, and His omniscience precludes the existence of any truly random event. The Bible does, however, use the word "chance" on occasion, but not as a completely unforeseen event. Here, chance generally indicates that the people involved had no way of knowing something would occur, but it doesn't follow that God didn't know.

The idea of luck brings up a difficult theological discussion: does God ordain everything that happens to us, or does he let nature and human choice play out to their inevitable end? The answer is a confusing "both." We do often bear the repercussions of choices—ours and others—without the apparent interference of God. In other cases, He acts in the form of "miracles." How, when, and why he acts are usually hidden from us but whether He ordained it or allowed it to happen is not in question. He is in control, orchestrating natural consequences and miracles in a way that will bring honour to Him and salvation to us.

What the Bible categorically condemns is the use of superstition to gain the favour of God. That being said, should a Christian own a lucky charm or engage in superstitious actions such as wearing the same socks to every baseball game? If the charms, such as a rabbit's foot, a horseshoe, or an elephant with an up-raised trunk are non-religious and used in a way that represents a culture and does not cause another to stumble or attempts to gather actual fortune, it's probably all right. Rituals can be used to calm nerves or mentally prepare for an event but we should all recognize that nothing is truly random, and God cannot be manipulated by four-leafed clovers or dirty socks. Time would be better spent by following God, preparing for the game, and not risking anything too dear in poker.[9]

"The Bible doesn't say, "Thou shall not play the lottery!"

So, does that mean the bible tolerates playing the lottery which is based on luck?

Perhaps not specifically but the Bible does, however, condemn gambling on its principles. What is the agenda of gambling? On the part of the Lottery Business, gambling's agenda is to feed on the public's greed, to increase ticket revenue as opposed to prize pay-out. On the part of the public, it aims to get as much money as possible for as little effort as possible.

The Bible speaks clearly on these things. Greed is covetousness, look at greed in the light of the scriptures: Romans 1:28-32 mentions it as "such a little sin?" It is mentioned here along with "haters of God". Ephesians 4:17-24 instructs us to no longer walk as those that are given over to greediness. 1 Timothy 6:10 says: to pursue "greediness" is to "stray from the faith". What about getting something for nothing? The picture of the lottery is getting everything you ever wanted without any effort. From the time that man was driven out of the garden we were told that we must work for our sustenance (Genesis 3:19). If a man does not work, he shouldn't eat (2 Thessalonians 3:10-12). There are people in this life that get things that they do not work for by taking advantage of others. They are called thieves. We are to work and receive our livelihood (1 Thessalonians 4:11).[10]

Such strong words clearly indicate great disdain for the lottery, the father of all luck, even for many believing Christians the mere saying of "good luck" is unbiblical, because God dictates what will and will not happen.

Luck in Islam

Islam is an Abrahamic monotheistic religion which teaches that Prophet Muhammad is a messenger of God. It is the world's second-largest religion with 1.9 billion followers comprising about 25 % of the world's population, known as Muslims. Muslims make up a majority of the population in 51 countries around the world. Most Muslim theologians and imams agree that there is no such thing as luck in Islam, despite the fact that the word Haz (Arabic for luck, good fortune) is mentioned numerous times in the Quran. They argue the word "Haz" in the Quran does not really mean luck, but it implies something else, like the measurable amount of something.

Everything and all things that happen in our life are predestined by Allah, the one and only creator. There is no such thing as good or bad luck according to Islam. When something good befalls you, it is not because you are an exceptional person. When something bad befalls you, it does not mean that you are cursed and are having a bout of "bad luck".

In Islam, everything happens for a reason, even though the reason may be imperceptible to us. Allah alone knows the wisdom behind it. The core of Islam is the notion that humans were created for one reason and that is to worship Allah Almighty. Everything else that happens is the mere icing on the cake and serves as a test as to who is the strongest in faith.

How many times have we seen someone win millions of dollars in a lottery windfall? Everyone around them laments about how lucky they are. However, we have also seen lottery winners suffer as a result of their win as they suffer from increased debt, family problems and sometimes even social stigmatization. So, the lottery win was not necessarily a good thing although it might superficially seem so.

While humans have been given their own free will, it must be understood that it does not circumvent or decrease Allah's ultimate will, which rules the universe and everything in it. Allah reveals in the Quran ''But you cannot will unless Allah wills; Allah is all-knowing, all-wise '' (The Quran 76:30).[11]

Luck and the concept of Qadar

Qadar in Islam means "the divine preordainment". The Quran states: ''Indeed, we have created all things with Qadar '' (The Quran 54:49), and since everything is preordained, luck does not really exist. There is no good or bad luck, but this idea of surrendering to Qadar does not clearly fit the commands in the Quran inciting believers to work and struggle as we see in The Quran 9:105. Take action! God will see your actions, as will His Messenger and the believers, and then you will be returned to Him who knows what is seen and unseen, and He will tell you what you have been doing.

This leads me to one fundamental question: is luck a tool used by Allah, is it a branch of Qadar? If so, does buying a lottery ticket, which is considered a sin in Islam, and actually winning a large sum of money mean Allah has preordained this massive win? How can the act then be considered a sin when it was already preordained?

Luck can't be found nor proven!

Al Azhar mosque, which is the centre of Sunni Islam in the world, has issued many fatwas declaring any game which depends on luck to be a sin. Thus, buying a lottery ticket is considered a sin as Al Azhar believes there is no such thing as luck. Grand Ayatollah Jafar Sobhani took a similar line and wrote that: ''The system of the universe is based on the law of cause and effect. Even the minutest happening is not an exception to this universal law.''

The roaring of the ocean, the falling of leaves, snowfall, rain, the difference in palm lines, variance in faces, the rise and fall of nations, social good and evil - each and every thing is bound by this law of cause and effect. Sometimes the reason is apparent and sometimes it is not. Therefore, there is no place for 'chance'. No philosophy of the world can prove the existence of 'chance', and to rely on chance is, in fact, to place trust in an imaginary thing, which is unrealistic.

Luck, accident, chance and fortune are all really superstitions. Only people who are unaware of the underlying causes of happenings mention them. They tend to believe in such things just to please their condemning conscience by trusting such unreal causes.

If we have to trust in 'chance', then we should say that only endeavour, work, struggle and activeness provide the basis of 'chance' and 'good luck'. This invisible cause lies behind activeness and hard work. Trust in luck is only an instrument for remaining idle and for misleading the mind. It is a tranquillizer for soothing the heart of idle and inactive persons. In other words, reliance on luck is a cover to conceal the conscience of sinners and wrongdoers.

If a player loses a game and the medal is awarded to someone else, he comes out of the playground with a dark face and a forehead wet with perspiration and in order to retrieve his loss tells his friends something like, "The luck of my rival was better. Hence, he won. This time my fortune was not good and therefore I lost." What is pitiable is that, by blaming luck, or his lack thereof, he does not find out the real reason for his failure, preventing future losses. Rather he resorts to imaginary causes, which have no basis from the viewpoint of knowledge, intelligence, philosophy or logic. Simply put – he refuses to take responsibility for his defeat.

The Holy Prophet's son Ibrahim passed away and there was a solar eclipse that very day. Superstitious people went to the Holy Prophet and said, "The calamity, which has befallen you, is so great that the sun too is mourning. This eclipse is due to the death of your dear son." In response, the Holy Prophet uttered this historical sentence, "O, people! Sun and moon do not mourn anybody's death. Rather, the lunar and solar eclipses are the signs of Allah's power. (The solar eclipse has a special reason. It should not be attributed to my son's demise)." [12]

Luck in Hinduism

According to many scholars, Hinduism is the world's oldest religion, with roots and customs dating back more than 4,000 years. Today, Hinduism is the third-largest religion behind Christianity and Islam, with about 900 million followers, of which roughly 95% live in India. Hinduism has its own understanding of luck. In Hinduism, every living being has a soul and according to Bhagwat Gita, this soul never dies. It reincarnates and takes rebirth. While living in one birth, the soul indulges in good and bad karmas (deeds). The reincarnation of the soul in the subsequent birth is determined by the quality and load of karmas of its previous birth. The following quote from Mahabharata is relevant: "Man is the dispenser of his own destiny. The actions done in a former life are seen to produce fruits in this. The soul is born again with its accumulated load of karmas. By performing only virtuous actions it attains to the state of the celestials. By a combination of good and bad actions, it acquires the state of human beings. By indulgence in sensuality and similar vices, it is born among the lower animals." (Mahabharata, III. 208.22.30).

This statement clarifies that rebirth in the human race is also a matter of luck. It depends upon the accumulated karmas of a soul's previous births. If it is born into a wealthy family, it is considered lucky and if it is reborn as a beggar, it will be considered unlucky.[13]

Lakshmi: The Hindu goddess of wealth, beauty and luck

For Hindus, the goddess Lakshmi symbolizes good luck. The word Lakshmi is derived from the Sanskrit word Laksya, meaning "aim" or "goal", and in the Hindu faith, she is the goddess of wealth and prosperity in material and spiritual forms. For most Hindu families, Lakshmi is the household goddess, and she is a particular favourite of women. Although she is worshipped daily, the festive month of October is Lakshmi's special month. Lakshmi Puja is celebrated on the full moon night of Kojagari Purnima, the harvest festival that marks the end of the monsoon season.

Lakshmi is said to be the daughter of the mother goddess Durga, and the wife of Vishnu, whom she accompanied during each of his incarnations, often taking different physical forms. Lakshmi symbolizes the active energy of Vishnu, and they often appear together as Lakshmi-Narayan - Lakshmi accompanying Vishnu.

Lakshmi is usually depicted as a beautiful woman with a golden complexion, with four hands, sitting or standing on a full-bloomed lotus and holding a lotus bud, which symbolises beauty, purity, and fertility. Her four hands represent the four ends of human life: dharma or righteousness, kama or desires, artha or wealth, and moksha or liberation from the cycle of birth and death. Cascades of gold coins are often seen flowing from her hands, suggesting that those who worship her will gain wealth. She always wears gold embroidered red clothes, where the red symbolizes activity, and the golden lining indicates prosperity.

Two elephants spraying water are often shown standing next to the goddess. This symbolises that ceaseless effort, when practised in accordance with one's dharma and governed by wisdom and purity, leads to both material and spiritual prosperity. To symbolize her many attributes, Lakshmi may appear in any of eight different forms, representing everything from knowledge to food grains.

The importance attached to the presence of Lakshmi in every household essentially makes her a domestic deity. Householders traditionally worship Lakshmi on a Friday as a symbol of the well-being and prosperity of the family. Businessmen and businesswomen also celebrate her as a symbol of prosperity and offer her daily prayers. On the full moon night following Dusshera or Durga Puja, Hindus worship Lakshmi ceremonially at home, pray for her blessings, and invite neighbours to attend the puja. It is believed that on this full moon night the goddess herself visits the homes and replenishes the inhabitants with wealth. Special worship is also offered to Lakshmi on the auspicious Diwali night, the festival of lights.[14]

Reading Lord Krishan words, it seems that luck can be earned indeed: "Destiny and human effort depend upon each other. The high-minded perform good and great deeds. It is only eunuchs who worship fate." (Mahabharata, XII. 139. 81).

Luck in Buddhism

Buddhism is an Indian religion based on a series of original teachings attributed to Gautama Buddha. It originated in ancient India as a Sramana tradition sometime between the 6th and 4th centuries BCE, spreading through much of Asia. Buddhism does not believe in luck. It believes all happenings or non-happenings must have a cause. Buddha believes that a lucky or unlucky event is the result of a specific cause and not due to luck, chance or fate.

Buddhists believe that good or bad luck is a result of past and present karmas and the logic is simple: good 'kamma' acts bring good 'kammic' outcomes. The force of this kammic outcome depends not so much on the actual act, but rather on how you felt in your heart while doing the deed. For example, giving away a £5 note to one needy person with a sincere and good heart is more effective than giving away £1000 with little soul or heart.

The Buddha emphasised that good luck is about training your mind to observe with clarity and to cherish your family and to help others. Developing your mind is more important than good fortune.

Low Arts

What about using magic to bring luck, or relying on fortune-telling? The Buddha considers practices such as fortune-telling, wearing magic charms for protection, fixing lucky sites for building or prophesizing and fixing lucky days to be useless superstitions and he expressly forbids his disciples to practice such things. He calls all these things 'low arts'. "Whereas some religious men, while living of food provided by the faithful, make their living by such low arts, such wrong means of livelihood as palmistry, divining by signs, interpreting dreams... bringing good or bad luck... invoking the goodness of luck... picking the lucky site for a building, the monk Gotama refrains from such low arts, such wrong means of livelihood." (D.I, 9-12).

In the teachings of the Buddha, it is honesty, kindness, understanding, patience, forgiveness, generosity, loyalty and other good qualities that truly protect you and give you prosperity.

The Buddha teaches us that it is far more important to develop our hearts and minds. He says: ''Being deeply learned and skilled; being well-trained and using well-spoken words - this is the best good luck. To support your mother and father, to cherish your wife and child and to have a simple livelihood; this is the best good luck. Being generous and just, helping one's relatives and being blameless in one's actions; this is the best good luck. To refrain from evil and from strong drink, and to be always steadfast in virtue; this is the best good luck. Reverence, humility, contentment, gratitude and hearing the good Dhamma; this is the best good luck. '' (Sn. 261-265 15).[15]

Luck in Chinese tradition

One of the most widely seen Chinese characters in China is 福 fú, the character for good fortune or luck. You see it painted as decoration everywhere: on wind chimes, paintings, lanterns, pots and posters. A look at its origin gives you feel for the complexity and longevity of symbols in Chinese culture. It also represents the God of Fortune (Fu), who is part of the good luck trinity of Fu, Lu and Shou (luck, prosperity and long life).

China has known many symbols and meanings which revolve around good fortune and luck. The Chinese believe that by filling their lives with lucky objects and images, they increase their prosperity and happiness, making their existence more joyful and fulfilling.

For centuries, symbols and written script have graced their impressive architecture, language, artwork, and everyday objects. Lucky images and symbols are used to create an environment that is protected from illness, bad fortune, and accidents.[16]

Fortune (Fú 福) Prosperity (Lù 禄) Longevity (Shòu 寿)

The Sanxing (三星 "Three Stars") are the gods of the three stars or constellations considered essential in Chinese astrology and mythology: Jupiter, Ursa Major, and Canopus. Fu, Lu, and Shou are also the embodiments of fortune, with Fu (Fortune) presiding over the planet Jupiter, Lu (Prosperity) presiding over

Ursa Major, and Shou (Longevity) presiding over Canopus. They have emerged from Chinese folk religion with their iconic representation as three, old, bearded, wise men dating back to the Ming dynasty when the gods of the three stars were represented in human form for the first time. They are sometimes identified with other deities of the Chinese religion of Taoism.[17]

The three stars are commonly used in Chinese culture to denote the three attributes of a good life. Statues of these three gods are found on the facades of folk religion's temples and ancestral shrines, in nearly every Chinese home and many Chinese-owned shops on small altars with a glass of water, and an orange or other auspicious offering, especially during Chinese New Year. Traditionally, they are arranged right to left (so Shou is on the left of the viewer, Lu in the middle, and Fu on the far right), just as Chinese characters are traditionally written from right to left.[18]

The three gods, their stars and their attributes

Fuxing

The star of Fu (福), Fuxing 福星, refers to the planet Jupiter. In traditional astrology, the planet Jupiter was believed to be fortunate. Alternatively, according to a Taoist myth of the Ming dynasty, the Fu star is associated with Yang Cheng (楊成), a governor of Daozhou in the Tang Dynasty. Yang Cheng risked his life by writing a memorial to the emperor to save the people from presenting dwarf slaves as a special tribute to the imperial court. After his death, the people built a temple to commemorate him, and over time he came to be considered the personification of good fortune.

He is generally depicted in scholar's dress, holding a scroll, on which is sometimes written the character "Fu". He may also be seen holding a child or surrounded by children. He is sometimes conflated with Caishen, the "Wealth God".

Luxing

The star of Lu (祿), Luxing 祿星 in traditional Chinese astronomy is the sixth star in the Wenchang cluster, and like the Fu star came to be personified as Zhang Xian who lived during the Later Shu dynasty. The word Lu specifically refers to the salary of a government official. As such, the Lu star is the star of prosperity, rank, and influence. The Lu star was also worshipped separately from the other two as the deity dictating one's success in the imperial examinations, and therefore success in the imperial bureaucracy. The Lu star is usually depicted in the dress of a mandarin.

Shouxing

The star of Shou (壽), Shouxing 壽星, is the star of the South Pole in Chinese astronomy and is believed to control the life span of mortals. According to legend, he was carried in his mother's womb for ten years before being born and was already an old man when delivered. He is recognized by his high, domed forehead and the peach which he carries as a symbol of immortality. This longevity god is usually shown smiling and friendly, and he may sometimes be carrying a gourd filled with the elixir of life. He is sometimes conflated with Laozi and corresponding gods of Taoist theology.[19]

The Japanese Seven Lucky Gods

In Japanese mythology, the Seven Lucky Gods or Seven Gods of Fortune (七福神, shichifukujin in Japanese) are believed to grant good luck and are often represented in netsuke and in artworks. One of the seven (Jurōjin) is said to be based on a historical figure. They all began as remote and impersonal gods, but gradually became more important canonical figures for certain professions and Japanese arts. During the course of their history, the mutual influence between the gods has created confusion about which of them was the patron of certain professions. The worship of this group of gods is also due to the importance of the number seven in Japan, supposedly a signifier of good luck.[20]

It is known that these deities mostly have their origins as ancient gods of fortune from religions popular in Japan such as Mahayana Buddhism (Benzaiten, Bishamonten, Daikokuten) which came to Japan from China but originated in India, and from Chinese Taoism (Fukurokuju, Hotei, Jurojin). Only one, Ebisu has a native Japanese ancestry. These gods have been recognized as such for over a thousand years. In the beginning, these gods were worshipped by merchants as the first two (Ebisu and Daikokuten) were gods of business and trade.

Subsequently, the other classes of Japanese society looked for other gods that could correspond with their professions: Benzaiten as the patron of the arts, Fukurokuju as the patron of the sciences, and so on. In ancient times, these gods were worshipped separately, but this rarely happens today – only when it is required for the god to act on behalf of the applicant. The Seven Gods of Fortune started being mentioned as a collective in the year 1420 in Fushimi, in order to imitate the processions of the daimyōs, the feudal lords of pre-modern Japan. It is said that the Buddhist priest Tenkai selected these gods after speaking with the shōgun he served, Iemitsu Tokugawa, at the order of seeking whoever possessed the perfect virtues: longevity, fortune, popularity, sincerity, kindness, dignity, and magnanimity.

During the first three days of the New Year, the Seven Lucky Gods are said to pilot through the heavens to human ports on the Takarabune or Treasure Ship.[21]

Luck in Ancient Egypt

The ancient Egyptians wrote calendars that marked lucky and unlucky days. These predictions were based on astronomical and mythological events thought of as influential to everyday life. The best preserved of these calendars is the Cairo Calendar, a papyrus document dating between 1163 and 1271 B.C. The entry for each day is prefaced by three hieroglyphics that indicate either good or bad luck, with the characters often derived from events of mythology. Astronomers at the University of Helsinki in Finland have previously discovered that some of the fortunate days recurred every 29.6 days. This almost exactly matches the length of the lunar cycle — the time between two full moons. Alternatively, new moons may have been associated with bad luck.

Scientists also detected another pattern in the calendar, one that occurred every 2.85 days, and researchers suggest this approximately matches the regular dimming of Algol, "the Demon Star," which lies approximately 93 light-years away in the constellation Perseus as one of the eyes of Medusa's head. Its name comes from the Arabic phrase, ra's al-ghul, which means "the demon's head"[22]

The calendar of lucky and unlucky days is based on the belief that Egyptian myths represent recurrent events that possibly have an effect on everyday life. Examples of this are the daily (night vs day) and yearly (aggressive vs weak) life cycles of the sun god and the seasonal flooding of the Nile. It is natural that these observed phenomena were considered of utmost importance to the well-being and fortune of the Egyptians. However, on the perspective of the calendars of lucky and unlucky days, the influence of the divine world upon man during any particular year is not restricted to only these major events. Mythological feast days, days of battle or peace between gods, days of the arrival of the winds, and days with a certain lucky or unlucky number were also equally important for understanding this type of divination. In the minds of the ancient Egyptians, gods' moods and attitudes were perceived to be directly visible and a tangible phenomenon. The understanding and knowledge of the proper place for every divine and mythological event in the yearly cycle, as it could be observed in nature, was a way to avoid the displeasure of the gods and thus an important social and religious issue for the Egyptians.[23]

Chapter 4
Luck And Fortune-Tellers

Luck And Fortune-Tellers

Bringing luck or just a witches' brew bubbling of lies and lizards?

Humans throughout the centuries sought the help of fortune tellers, witches and lizards to bring good luck and to foresee the future in an attempt to avoid bad luck. I am contemplating the concept of luck in terms of fortune-tellers. I find it fitting to furnish the reader with the basics of this strange and foggy world. By understanding different practices and rituals that are supposed to bring good luck and fortune, we can also understand more about luck itself and how different cultures around the world utilize witchcraft, magic and sorcery to bring lasting bliss and fortune.

The mere use of witchcraft indicates that luck was viewed as an unseen paranormal force that exists somewhere beyond our physical reach, and by only calling on the spirits' help, it could be brought into our life!

Terminology[1234]

Witchcraft is the practice whereby a witch casts spells and performs magical rituals with the use of supernatural skills and abilities. It is a broad term that has varied meanings in different cultures and societies, so it remains somewhat difficult to define. The most common understanding of witchcraft in most cultures, notably in Africa and the African diaspora, Asia, Latin America and indigenous nations in the Americas, is that it is evil and it harms the innocent.

In the Philippines, witches are seen as those opposed to the sacred. In contrast, anthropologists writing about the healers in indigenous Philippine religions either use the traditional terminology of these cultures or broad anthropological terms like "shaman" to refer to witches.

Belief in witchcraft is often present within societies and groups whose cultural framework includes a magical worldview. In the modern era, some may use "witchcraft" to refer to benign, positive, or neutral metaphysical practices that include divination, meditation, or self-help techniques found in modern Pagan and New Age movements. This reversal in nomenclature is primarily a modern, Western, and pop culture phenomenon, most prevalent amongst the youth and adherents of modern Pagan traditions like Wicca. When talking about witchcraft, people often refer to being 'jinxed' or being under a spell of "voodoo".

Despite all of this, witchcraft is certainly real and many witches paid for their special gifts at the stake. Today many cultures around the world still embrace witchcraft in its various forms - sorcery, dark magic, voodoo, and more.

The word voodoo originated from the Louisiana French voudou, which is related to the African word for a spirit or deity (vódũ). For many, the word conjures up an old serial image of a witch doctor sticking pins in a doll, while miles away an innocent, unwitting victim suffers in pain. Some think of zombies stalking the earth in search of human blood. With the tendency to associate voodoo with evil, it may surprise some to learn that it is a religion that combines elements of Roman

Catholic rituals with elements of native African religions and magic.

Mojo is a magical word with African voodoo roots that refers to spells, hexes, or charms. The word is related to the Gullah creole word moco, meaning "witchcraft, magic," and the Fulani word moco'o meaning "medicine man". Nowadays, mojo has more to do with working personal charm and charisma than with working voodoo magic.

Fortune-telling is the practice of predicting information about a person's life. The scope of fortune-telling is in principle identical with the practice of divination. The difference is that divination is the term used for predictions considered part of a religious ritual, invoking deities or spirits. Alternatively, the term fortune-telling implies a less serious or informal setting, even one of popular culture, where belief in occult workings behind the prediction is less prominent than the concept of suggestion, spiritual or practical advisory or affirmation.

Contemporary Western images of fortune-telling grew out of the folkloristic reception of Renaissance magic commonly associated with the Romani people. During the 19th and 20th centuries, methods of divination from non-Western cultures, such as the I Ching, were also adopted as methods of fortune-telling in western popular culture. There is opposition to fortune telling in Christianity, Islam, and Judaism based on scriptural prohibitions against divination.

Terms for one who claims to see into the future include fortune teller, crystal-gazer, spaewife, seer, soothsayer, sibyl, clairvoyant, and prophet. Related terms among other abilities include oracle, augur, and visionary. Fortune telling is dismissed by the scientific community and scientific sceptics as being based on magical thinking and superstition.

Divination (from the Latin divinare, 'to foresee, to foretell, to predict, to prophesy', related to divinus, 'divine'), or "to be inspired by a god", is the attempt to gain insight into a question or situation by way of an occultic, standardized process or ritual. Used in various forms throughout history, diviners ascertain their interpretations of how a querent should proceed by reading signs, events, or omens, or through alleged contact with a supernatural agency. Divination can be seen as a systematic method with which to organize what appears to be disjointed, random facets of existence such that they provide insight into a problem at hand. If a distinction is to be made between divination and fortune-telling, divination has a more formal or ritualistic element and often contains a more social character, usually in a religious context, as seen in traditional African medicine. Fortune-telling, on the other hand, is a more everyday practice for personal purposes. Divination methods vary by culture and religion.

Divination has long been criticized by society. In the modern era, it has been dismissed by the scientific community and sceptics as being superstitious as experiments do not support the idea that divination techniques can predict the future more reliably or precisely than would be possible without it.

A psychic is a person who claims to use extrasensory perception (ESP), particularly involving telepathy or clairvoyance, to identify information hidden from the normal senses. They are also known for performing acts that are inexplicable by natural laws. Although many people believe in psychic abilities, the scientific consensus is that there is no proof of the existence of such powers. Science thus describes these practices as pseudoscience. The word "psychic" is also used as an adjective to describe psychic abilities.

Psychics encompass people in a variety of roles. Some are theatrical performers, such as stage magicians, who use various techniques such as prestidigitation, cold reading, and hot reading to produce the appearance of psychic abilities for entertainment purposes. A large industry and network exist whereby people advertised as psychics provide advice and counsel to clients. Some famous psychics include Edgar Cayce, Ingo Swann, Peter Hurkos, Janet Lee, Jose Ortiz El Samaritano, Miss Cleo, John Edward, Sylvia Browne, and Tyler Henry. Psychic powers are asserted by psychic detectives in practices such as psychic archaeology and even psychic surgery.

Psychics are sometimes featured in science fiction and fantasy fiction. Examples of fiction featuring characters with psychic powers include the Star Wars franchise that features "Force-sensitive" beings that can see into the future and move objects telekinetically. Other examples include Dungeons & Dragons and some of the works of Stephen King amongst many others.

Clairvoyance is the claimed ability to gain information about an object, person, location, or physical event through extrasensory perception. Any person who is claimed to have such ability is said to be a clairvoyant ("one who sees clearly"). Claims for the existence of paranormal and psychic abilities such as clairvoyance have not been supported by scientific evidence. Parapsychology explores this possibility, but the existence of the paranormal is not accepted by the scientific community.

A psychic reading is a specific attempt to discern information through the use of heightened perceptive abilities or natural extensions of the basic human senses of sight, sound, touch, taste and instinct. These natural extensions are claimed to be clairvoyance (vision), clairsentience (feeling), Clair cognisance (factual knowing) and clairaudience (hearing) and the resulting statements made during a reading. Psychic reading is considered a pseudoscience and a cold reading technique that allows psychics to produce seemingly specific information about an individual from social cues and broad statements.

Palmistry, also known as palm reading, chiromancy or chirology, is the practice of fortune-telling through the study of the palm. The practice is found all over the world, with numerous cultural variations. Those who practice chiromancy are generally called palmists or hand readers.

The difference between a psychic and a witch is that a psychic is a person who possesses, or appears to possess, extra-sensory abilities such as precognition, clairvoyance and telepathy, or one who appears to be susceptible to paranormal or supernatural influence while a witch is a person who practices witchcraft.

The magic of superstition, witches, and potions

Humans are captivated by magic, myth and the unknown. Magic speaks to our imagination, our romantic notion, and our sense of adventure. It is no surprise then that we embrace so many mythical symbols that include stones, leaves, dwarves, butterflies, flowers, bugs, stars, horses, rabbits, leprechauns, statues, elves, fairies and witches, storytellers and many more. People can become obsessed with lucky charms and would wear them, revere them and or consult them for direction, luck, and fortune.

Sometimes these symbols and objects have increased significance due to superstitions about their luck and fortune. Someone would carry a four-leaf clover in their pocket when buying a lotto ticket or would wear an "evil-eye" necklace to bring them luck or to keep bad luck at bay. In some cases, these symbols have more meaning than life itself and those who embrace them can even feel lost without them.

Humans are spiritual beings and the aura of mysticism will captivate most people to some extent. There are, of course, people who do not put any value on myth, would not pray to Buddha to heal an illness and would not care if the last seat in the house is number 13. The reality is that many people have superstitions and hold on to things that speak to their innermost self. Our special believes or fascinations can easily cross the line into obsession - like when that lizard is no longer a lizard but becomes a spirited animal with magic powers, almost like a wizard with powers that can change our destiny.

Those with strong imaginations consume books about science-fiction and the supernatural, such as the likes of Harry Potter, The Wizard of Oz and Hocus Pocus to mention but a few. Both children and adults love them and some people collect them. These fantasy books are tailor-made to suit our penchant for magic, fantasy and imaginary characters who live charmed lives far removed from our own.

We create our own imaginary world and we can write our own stories with whimsical leprechauns, witches, wizards, lizards, fairies, and elves. Marvel is not limited to the over-imaginative mind. There is, however, a thin line between fanciful and fixation and we can attach too much value to what is simply a clover leaf, a number, a star, a gemstone, or a statue. For those who turn to the mystique for their spiritual guidance, the fantasy is real and the meaning they derive from marvel and magic becomes their reality.

Life is often relentlessly hard and it is easier to escape into fantasy than dealing with what is in front of us. There is so much mystique and fantasy associated with fairy-tale characters and objects that people are easily charmed by them. Even numbers have significant innuendos attached to them, for example: The number seven stands for perfection, there are seven days in a week, rainbows have seven colours, seven has a significance in many religions, triple seven is significant in games of chance, there are similar beliefs and superstitions about the number eight.

Luck is an intention set in motion. Does that mean we choose our luck? It seems as if many people turn to symbols, objects, and other sources for their slice of fortune. Many consults with fortune-tellers for love, luck, and many other things. Others base their luck and desires on the marvels of leprechauns, leaves, little statues, and elves. A rock, crystal, magic potion or even a certain colour or outfit has a special meaning and purpose for some – carrying a special message about how things will turn out.

Throughout history witches, lizards and fortune tellers have been associated with luck or even ill luck. Many engaged wizards and witches for life decisions. I am not so sure that I will consult a witch with her cat and magic potion for my next life decision, but presi and kings have called upon their powers for centuries and will keep on doing so for some time to come.

William Shakespeare had a different opinion about witches when he quoted: "Thunder. Enter the three witches. Double, double, toil and trouble; fire burn, and cauldron bubble". He certainly had witchcraft on his mind: -Ay, that incestuous, that adulterate beast, with witchcraft of his wit, with traitorous gifts- O wicked wit and gifts, that have the power to seduce! Let witchcraft join with beauty, lust with both!

And:

Double, double toil and trouble;

Fire burn and caldron bubble.

Fillet of a fenny snake,

In the caldron boil and bake;

Eye of newt and toe of frog,

Wool of bat and tongue of dog,

Adder's fork and blind-worm's sting,

Lizard's leg and howlet's wing,

For a charm of powerful trouble,

Like a hell-broth boil and bubble.

Double, double toil and trouble;

Fire burn and caldron bubble.

Cool it with a baboon's blood,

Then the charm is firm and good.

Macbeth: IV.i 10-19; 35-38

William Shakespeare[5]

Why did Shakespeare use witches in all his tales, despite their trouble, bubble, and blood? Just like the rest of society, he was lost in dark magic and suspense. Strange then that these magical creatures called witches have always been depicted as old and ugly women without all their teeth and puckered faces. In films and books, they are pictured as ugly, horrible, and scary and they are the subject of nightmares for many a little one, rather than a whimsical fantasy. Witches were often feared and many were burned at the stake as they must have brought about some ill luck or at least ill will to many who feared them and wanted them dead.

William Shakespeare's superstitious about witches were depicted in many of his books. He wrote the story of Macbeth specially to appeal to King James during his rule as king. The three witches in Macbeth manipulated the characters into disaster and cast spells to destroy lives. People were very superstitious in those days. They blamed plagues, deaths, and unpleasant illness on the work of witches. Thus, famous books and plays such as Macbeth, Hamlet, The Tempest and Julius Caesar were inspired by the supernatural and witchcraft in particular.

Shakespeare had many ghosts, witches, floating daggers, and prophetic spirits as characters in his plays. He presented their images as calm versus threatening to add depth to various scenes with powerful messages as a result. Julius Caesar depicted omens from a soothsayer (fortune teller) to warn people of terrible things to come. Shakespeare used witchery to build suspense and keep his audience captive and his work is still important up to this day.[6]

The history of witches and witchcraft

The concept of witches and witchcraft is centuries old. It was especially predominant in Shakespeare's lifetime; he was fascinated with witches and saw them as interesting story material. The idea of witchcraft was brought to the forefront through Shakespeare's work. All evil and ill were contributed to witches, witchcraft, demons, and the devil. Witches were responsible for the fate of sick animals, crops that did not grow and plagues in villages. Those accused of being witches were old, poor and single women and they were often mistreated in their communities.

The idea of witches on broomsticks originated from this ancient era and is still a popular phenomenon today. If a woman was suspected of being a witch, she was caught, tied up and put into water. If she floated, she was a confirmed a witch and she was burnt. The alternative meant sinking and drowning. This was just one form of cruelty against witches who were ironically revered by many. The killing of witches was done following laws passed in ancient times. Then again, people held onto many superstitions such as not walking under ladders, viewing black cats as unlucky and being destined for bad luck if you lose your hair, to mention a few.

The history of witches and witchcraft originated before the Christian world, in a time where both intellectuals and ordinary people embraced the idea of witches, witchcraft, elves, and demons from a murky underworld. Witchcraft was not limited to England but was also prominent in ancient Roman times and archaeologists found 'curse tablets' in graves, wells and fountains believed to be from this time. Witches are featured predominately in classical literature and witchcraft is still practised all over the world today.

We grow up with the notion of a witch as an ugly stick figure in a long black cloak stirring a boiling pot over an open fire with a pole almost the size of her nose. I am not sure if it relates to their magical powers or just the fear of the unknown, but superstition featured heavily in the makeup of their history.

Witches are often portrayed with black cats. It was believed that witches could separate parts of themselves and send this 'likeness' to others to do magic on their behalf. They are believed to have supernatural powers that enable them to control humans and nature. One of the more popular forms of good witchcraft is the practice of putting a "love spell" on people to bring them happiness or love.

As humans, we seek reasons for good or bad luck. If someone has extreme good or bad luck, we attach some supernatural power to it. Maybe in ancient times, people were looking for someone to blame for all the plagues and pandemics, disasters and poverty and witches were just in the line of fire.

People who look different are often the victims of witch trials:-

- In Tanzania, albino people are in danger of being killed for their skin and body parts. Since 2007, more than 50 albinos have been killed for ritual use. Tanzanian witch doctors believe the arms, legs, skin, and hair of albinos have a special magic in them, and that their use will bring their clients good luck in love, life, and business. Additionally, about 500 elderly women are being murdered each year in Tanzania following accusations of witchcraft or witchery.

- In the Republic of Benin, the country's government has used people's fears of witchcraft to explain why some people fair better than others. According to many legends, a baby that is not born head-first and with its face upwards is considered to be a witch. The so-called baby witches have been blamed for poor agricultural seasons or illnesses. Many babies are abandoned or killed as a consequence.

- President Yahya Jammeh of Gambia believed he was being targeted by witches. According to Amnesty International, as many as 1,000 Gambians accused of witchcraft have been arrested and tortured on orders from the president, which resulted in the death of some. President Jammeh also claims to be able to cure AIDS on Thursdays and fires doctors who disagree with him as reported by Mary Schons in the National Geographic.

- Belief in witchcraft continues to be present today in some societies and accusations of witchcraft are the trigger for serious forms of violence, including murder. Such incidents are common in countries such as Burkina Faso, Ghana, India, Kenya, Malawi, and Nepal.[7]

Accusations of witchcraft are sometimes linked to personal disputes, jealousy, and conflicts between neighbours or family members over land or inheritance.

Sometimes children are believed to be "possessed by devils" or to emit evil powers and they are used as witches. Child spiritual abuse is not new and as recently as 2017-2018, 1630 cases of "faith-based abuse" were investigated against children in England.

Being a witch became a crime in the late 1400s mostly due to abuse of the craft. Those found guilty were executed. In 1736 the law changed and witchcraft was no longer illegal in Britain. Huge numbers of people continued to believe in it, but just as many people were afraid of witches and continue to persecute and even murder them.

Faith is powerful and the placebo effect is real. Belief and positive thinking can work magic or at least wonders. Some people find magical rituals psychologically therapeutic and as such witchcraft, both good and bad, will probably be with us for long time to come.

Fortune telling

People contemplate the future and most of us wonder what is in stall for us. We want to know the 'unknowable'. Some gaze at stars or find patterns in clouds, others inspect metals or animals and some offer their hands, feet and faces to people who read patterns, to show us what we do not know.

The Romans are closely associated with fortune-telling and the 'drabardi' (Romany soothsayers) offered their services on all street corners. The image of the drabardi was so well-known and widespread that it became synonymous with fortune-telling, making its way into popular culture through films, books, pictures and even board games.

The nomadic Roma was responsible for taking the art of palmistry – reading lines and undulations on the palm– to every corner of Europe. It became so popular in the Middle Ages that witch hunters used birthmarks and other marks on the palm as proof of a satanic pact, and its popularity endured through the scientific and artistic revolutions of the Renaissance, although with a touch of scepticism. The Italian painter Caravaggio's 1595 masterpiece The Fortune Teller tells a story of a drabardi reading a naive young man's palm - stealing his gold ring while she does it.

Another widespread form of predicting the future is tasseomancy - literally meaning "divination of the cup" - the practice of telling fortunes by looking at the shapes left by tea leaves or coffee grounds in the bottom of a cup. It thrived in Eastern Europe, probably brought there by Sufi mystics from Turkey who believed that drinking coffee awakened the brain and opened it to new forms of vision.[8]

In Britain, tea first arrived from China in the mid-1600s and with it the practice of reading tea leaves. The legend around the inside of a charming teacup from Stoke on Trent in England reads: "Many curious things I see when telling fortunes in your tea". There were even how-to manuals for do-it-yourself divination. The shape of a dove for instance meant prosperity and luck. A chair in the teacup meant imminent pregnancy, and anyone finding three women at the bottom of their cup was about to become mixed up in a terrible scandal.

Playing cards arrived in Europe in the 15th century, and it was not long before they were used to tell fortunes. Tarot cards were another popular form of fortune-telling known as 'cartomancy'. The 'Oracle' tarot cards were designed, drawn and hand-painted by Mage Edmond, a 19th-century clairvoyant whose clients included Napoleon III. The cards mix celestial bodies like the Sun, Moon and Venus with ancient Egyptian symbols and classic tarot cards like the Tower. His deck was widely copied and is still used by many 'readers' today.

But not all forms of European fortune telling have ancient roots. The Ouija board was invented in America in the late 19th century but drew heavily on European traditions of spiritualism. One type of board went on sale in London in 1893 and was marketed as fun family entertainment with a paranormal element. It was not until 1973, when the Ouija board scene in the horror film The Exorcist terrified audiences so much, that it gained a spookier reputation and sales plummeted.

Fortune telling is possibly as old as the existence of mankind. People have always been fascinated by future predictions, but fortune-telling is not just an institution for those who want details about their future as it also plays a part in religion and medicine. In a religious context, fortune tellers are called prophets and prophets often gave their people very important directives, warnings, and predictions about future events.

Fortune telling has also long been associated with gipsies – a people who have often been outcasts in many different societies and unfortunately, still carry a stigma today. The origin of gipsies is quite hard to trace. Some believe they had origins in India, some think they originated in Egypt and others believe they hail from Turkey. Scholars, however, have studied their language and dialect and believe that their home was most likely Romania.

Rulers and kings in medieval times would often seek fortune tellers to predict events surrounding their kingdom. Popular methods included reading tea leaves, palms, astrology, and consulting tarot cards.

In some eastern countries, fortune-telling is respected as part of the community's personal and business life and people call upon clairvoyants for most of their decisions. The practice is not limited to the East as many Western nations consult with fortune tellers in both a management consulting and spiritual capacity.

Evidence indicates that forms of fortune-telling were practised in ancient China, Egypt, Chaldea, and Babylonia. In Thailand people rely heavily on fortune-telling and astrology for anything from personal guidance to the choice of their leaders. The King has his special troupe of psychics, guiding him through readings and astrology. As I mentioned in earlier chapter, these 'royal astrologers' make predictions about all future events and leaders rely heavily on their contributions.[9]

We all want an optimistic forecast and positive karma, which is why fortune-tellers capitalize on the concept. Most fortune-tellers will not share bad news and they will probably tell you what you want to hear. No wonder they are believed to be the source of good luck – they promise us that "good fortune will be ours".

Are fortune-tellers visionaries or perhaps normal people with learned psychic abilities who gaze into our future and take a guess on a probable outcome? If we think about fortune-tellers and gipsies, they conjure up bright colours, polished crystal balls and yellow caravans with bright designs. We do not envision dark rooms with sombre ladies in black attire. If the messages were all sombre, we would not seek them. We want to hear good news and the message of luck and fortune is really what interests us most.

Both the Rolling Stones (1962) and Maroon 5 (more recently) - recorded songs with the title "Fortune Teller". Perhaps the lyrics in these songs can tell us exactly what to expect when we have our fortunes "read":

Fortune Teller – The Rolling Stones

Went to the fortune teller

Had my fortune read

I didn't know what to tell her

I had a dizzy feeling in my head

When she took a look at my palm

She said son are you feeling kinda warm?

And she looked into her crystal ball

And said you're in love

I said I could not be so

I'm not passionate with the girls I know

She said when the next one arrives

You'll be looking into her eyes

I left there in a hurry

Looking forward to my big surprise

The next day I discovered

That the fortune-teller told me lies

I hurried back down to that woman

As mad as I could be

I told her I didn't see nobody

Why'd she made a fool out of me

Then something struck me

As if it came from up above

While... [10]

Fortune Teller – Maroon 5

I'm not a fortune teller, I won't be bringing news

Of what tomorrow brings, I'll leave that up to you

I'm not a fortune teller, don't have crystal ball

I can't predict the future, can't see nothing at all

It doesn't mean I'm afraid of all the things that you say

But I just think we should stay stuck in the moment today

And as the seasons roll back, no matter how hard I try

Summer will end and the leaves will turn again

I don't know why you're acting like this

I don't know why you have to do it again

Why'd you have to go and ruin the night

Don't worry about tomorrow's mess

I never know how the future will go

I don't know what to tell you, I'm not a fortune teller

I never change, but I want you to stay

I don't know what to tell you, I'm not a fortune teller... [11]

Famous fortune tellers and their predictions

There are a few famous fortune-tellers who predicted current life events in previous centuries: The Greek priestess Le Pythia predicted wars and provided answers for various problems. Nostradamus predicted current events in the 1500s. Also known as Michel de Nostredame, published a book back in 1555 in France that claimed to predict numerous future events through poems. Some people say there is nothing to them, and that when translated properly, they show the reader vague predictions that can be very loosely interpreted and applied to many things. Others, however, say the man was a genius with a clear gaze into the future. Some say Nostradamus foretold the great fire of London that took place in 1666, the French Revolution, Louis Pasteur's work as the godfather of vaccines, the rise of Adolf Hitler, the bombing of Hiroshima and Nagasaki, JFK's assassination, and September 11th, 2001, to name a few. Not bad for one mind and one book.

Höffern, von Höffer or von Hoeffer (fl. 1722), was a German noblewoman and fortune teller. She became famous in Sweden during the first half of the 18th century, where she was called the first famous fortune-teller in Stockholm.

The success of Oprah Winfrey's career was predicted by psychic Jean Dixon. Dixon began her career as an astrologist writing in a syndicated column in newspapers in the 1900s in the United States. She wrote several best-selling books, including an astrological cookbook and horoscopes for animals. Like many other modern-day psychics, Dixon famously predicted President John F. Kennedy's assassination. She also advised President Franklin D. Roosevelt during WWII, and advised Richard Nixon while in office, on the topic of terrorism on U.S soil. Dixon had a wide audience and according to Oprah, she foretold her successful career and fame to come in a conversation back in 1977.

Daniel Dunglas Home lived in the 1800s in the United States and made his name by healing the sick and communicating with the dead of family and friends of his clients. He was originally from Scotland but moved to the United States as a child and went on to become a well-known physical medium and self-professed clairvoyant who gained fame with the elite on the east coast. He was famous for his so-called ability to let spirits speak directly through him. He also gained a following for his ability to levitate. Tables would dance in his presence, and history has it that he is said to have even levitated his own body to the ceiling in some séances. Many called Home a fraud steeped in trickery, but others backed his act, claiming it to be tried and true magic.

Edgar Cayce felt so at home while in a self-induced sleep state that he claimed his subconscious mind would leave his body and travel to the land of the spirits where it would collect knowledge about the future. It would then bring this back to the land of the living, where he would pass it onto his clients. Some say Cayce predicted the stock market crash of 1929 that led to the Great Depression. He is also said to have foretold World War II, the shifting of the Earth's magnetic poles, the collapse of the Soviet Union and an alliance occurring between the United States and Russia.

Do you think you need a great pair of eyes to see what others cannot? Perhaps it depends on your definition of "sight". One of the most famous clairvoyants in Bulgaria was Baba Vanga or Grandmother Vanga. Born with proper eyesight, she is said to have gradually lost it after suffering through a large natural disaster best described as a tornado. She says it lifted her and threw her a great distance. The injuries she sustained when hitting the ground caused her to slowly lose her eyesight. Baba Vanga is said to have predicted 9/11, Brexit, Thailand's tsunami of 2004, future time travel in 2304. Was she truly gifted with intelligence beyond the norm, or did she simply have a wild imagination?[12]

Predicting Luck and Future

The age-old tradition of divining the future has been practised for many centuries. Fortune tellers or clairvoyants, readers, psychics, and mediums - as they are generally referred to - use various means of predicting the future. This includes reading palms, interpreting dreams, using crystal balls or tarot cards, astrology or using animals, minerals, or numbers. These different methods are all used in search of destiny or disaster for those who consult them. What we are told by these predictions offer a small glimpse into the future. Fortune-tellers on average stray from sharing very bad news. Realistically, a fortune teller cannot know much about their 'clients' other than what they see in front of them, the 'aura' they perceive or read or the clues they gather from their specific methods.

Any person can open a pack of tarot cards, shuffle them, and pick several cards with different themes. If there is a lucky card, you might want to believe that there is luck in your future. It could be a powerful play on your mind and perhaps cause a psychic shift towards luck. You might subconsciously lean towards luck as a consequence and perhaps be fortunate as a result sometime in the future.

Some readers use a person's name or the specific letters in a name to provide clues about their future while some psychics use dream analysis to predict the future and quality of luck.

108

Fortune tellers can hold a high social position, especially those that work for government officials, big bosses and kings. Not every fortune-teller, however, works for billionaires. Some do not say a word while practising, those whose business completely relies on talking. Some need to be good-looking, great with words, incredibly smart and trained specifically to make huge business deals. To some extent, they are like psychologists, helping people solve their problems by giving advice. They also have to be good at statistics, for many "predictions" are based on these. Professional fortune-tellers work in a master and apprentice system, divided by factions. Like many underground organizations, each faction has its own codes to follow.

How do fortune tellers learn about your past and future?

The Chinese fortune-tellers or suanming shifu are very good at reading facial expressions and body language. They can also guess which topics interest you and can then make ambiguous conclusions. The major steps in a Chinese fortune telling session are normally as follows:

They get your attention by making ambiguous statements that can apply to anything about your life, career, relationships, wellbeing, etc. while trying to convince you to stay and listen to them. According to the words that caught your attention, they dig deeper and get to know you, potentially obtaining your trust, once they know what you are curious about, they make conclusions or raise questions that you desperately want to know the answers to. When you become anxious and seek advice to improve your future, they start to provide suggestions and ask for money. Some fortune-tellers may even get information about your personal history through your friends, relatives, or other means, to trick you into thinking they are psychics or have supernatural powers. History repeats itself, and peoples' past behaviour is often the best predictor of their future, thus the more they know about your past, the better they can guess your future. This practice is thus more psychological than magical.[13]

Why are there so many blind fortune tellers in China?

Films and literature often portray fortune-tellers as blind, and in real life, many of them will say they lost their vision because they gave away the secrets of heaven and were punished by God. In some ways, their blindness is an advantage when they are convincing clients of their powers since they cannot observe facial expressions or body features.

There is a possibility that fortune-telling is not total nonsense. Many fortune-telling methods and theories rely heavily on memory and require a "peaceful heart". Due to their lack of vision, the blind can focus and calculate well and are therefore good candidates for studying and passing on fortune-telling methods. There is also a main faction in the Chinese fortune-telling master and apprentice system called the blind faction. On the other hand, we have to consider the possibility that people who lost their sight still need to make a living, so they learn to be fortune-tellers.[14]

The psychology of fortune-telling

Whatever form the fortune-telling takes, the basic process is the same: seeking meaning through random patterns by employing one or a variety of methods, and drawing conclusions from the results. This method is also used in psychology where people are shown images and asked to define them. One example is the Rorschach test which leaves a lot up to impromptu interpretation. A person might even alter their results as the images shared can reflect things about themselves which they do not want to reveal. Fortune telling often comes down to imagination, a desired outcome, interpretation, and fabrication.

I believe fortune-telling remains a pseudoscience, as not everything you hear from fortune tellers can be deemed accurate. As in the case of all other 'professions', there will be experts and there will be imposters. If you want to know if you will be lucky in the future, do everything you humanly can, to make it so. That would be more of a trusted method towards the outcome.

So much of what we feel, believe and "see" is emotive and not cognitive. That saying "it is in the mind" is not something we should scoff at. A simple illustration could be getting a diagnosis from a medical doctor that you are dying of a deadly disease. Even though the doctor could have made a mistake by switching test results meaning you received the wrong diagnosis, you will start feeling very ill. The seed of doom was 'planted' and your body will react accordingly. We certainly can't deny the importance of mind over matter.

Fortune telling is based on this concept. If your reading is very positive and there is love and money in your near future, you will start looking for it around every corner. The seed was planted and the mind does the rest. It could very well be that love and money was in your destiny at this point, but if it so happens that you inherit richness in a few weeks and meet your forever person, you will trust your medium for the prediction. Our minds are powerful and we usually believe what we want to believe.

Some experts have insights into the future in terms of financial trends, but they analyse their predictions scientifically using financial data over extended periods. They can predict where the markets will go, and that is far from guesswork as it is based on current market trends and serious analysis. Getting financial guidance from a medium might not be the best idea. Your luck might just be a "Fillet of a fenny snake, In the caldron boil and bake" (Shakespeare)

We are responsible for what we do and the actions we take towards making our dreams a reality. You might write your future prediction on a piece of paper yourself, burn it and pray for good luck. The outcome could very well be the same as visiting a stranger with a crystal ball who will give you a random forecast and a massive bill.

If you feel out of luck in your life, a psychic is not necessarily going to change that. Resolving some anxiety and fear about your current circumstances could probably be best done with a real therapist. Giving you general advice about your life could even be provided by a close loyal friend who knows you better than a stranger. But there is no shortage of available mediums who will give you a variety of predictions that might become true in the future. You might just get the comfort that your luck would not change anytime soon and take consolation in that.

A good psychologist might work with real reasons holding you back from success, luck, and fortune. The reasons for failure could be linked to your beliefs, behaviour and habits. It might be advantageous to spend the money on a professional who will work with you to unearth your potential and guide you to fulfilling your dreams and wishes.

Is fortune telling just hocus-pocus?

Why do people hold on to the predictions of fortune-tellers when the predictions are often irrelevant and off course? Are we looking for luck and love in the wrong places? If you read up on the history of some fortune-tellers, it is clear that most of them learn their art. It could all just be a show. You might leave your destiny in the hands of someone who is preying on your desire to have luck, love and a happy life and taking advantage of your vulnerable state.

I believe that fortune-telling is based on simple principles: awareness, instinct, observation, deduction plus the art of telling people what they want to hear. Whilst asking simple questions and shuffling cards, a reader can deduce basic information about a client and "make up" a prediction that seems plausible – something with good fortune, good health with just a little warning thrown into the mix to make it more convincing. It would not be difficult to achieve – it is a ritual that can be repeated with different people and none would be the wiser. Add some props, a colourful tablecloth, a shiny crystal ball and a much-used deck of tarot cards, dimmed lighting and the stage is set to change people's fortunes.

In short, fortune-telling is about possibilities rather than the truth, and many are exploited by those who prey on our vulnerability and our desire to have better outcomes.

Those who see fortune-tellers regularly will be able to recognize some of the standard readings - "You will meet a tall, dark stranger!" It is never stated how or where this person would appear, what he would look like, how you will recognize him and if he would be sans a mental illness.

Does fortune telling bring good or bad luck?

If you keep visiting psychics to obtain luck, it will probably cost a fortune and that in itself is not fortunate. Some people visit fortune tellers all the time, even for the smallest detail, and find that with time they are not able to make any decisions on their own. There is even a name for it – fortune teller addiction.

We do not know what the future holds – good or bad. Mankind is currently going through a crisis with a serious pandemic. I wonder how many psychics had Covid-19 in their forecast, and even if they did, they would not have been able to prevent it. The question about the validity of statements can be asked time after time - why can they predict certain things and the rest of it remains uncovered? Imagine if there was an accurate prediction of the current pandemic and mankind was able to stop it at the first infection. But no one had that insight and we now find ourselves in the middle of a very large global crisis that was not noted in any cards, tea leaves or crystal balls.

Are fortune tellers just "fortune readers" and not "fortune predictors"? They could, after all, just tell us what we want to hear. Are they just reading a certain card or tealeaf and making an estimated guess about how that "image" will play out in our immediate future? That is definitely not an accurate assessment of future reality. Maybe they can only see part of it, which is still not all of it but just a glimpse into the unknown. Even if you get a specific reading from your fortune teller, it might still exclude key facts about your life and future. Disaster may still await you around the next corner.

Can your fortune teller predict with all certainty that you will be lucky? If luck equals chance, then he/she is just making unreliable conjectures about your life and future which, is a very dangerous thing to do. Someone might just decide to gamble out all their money because they were told they are going to win a fortune. It is equal to leading a troupe of soldiers into battle and telling them they will win the war. There is just no certainty about anything lying ahead.

Does anyone really know how my life will turn out? Any decision and action I take today can drastically change my future. We live life with great uncertainty and we do not have insight into what lies ahead. I wonder why we want to know – we might hear things that will irrevocably change our lives and put us in danger.

If I seek an answer to a big decision or which course to take, a certain fortune-teller assure me that I am on the right track, but I would have to agree with that advice. If I align with her reading, I will have more confidence with what lies ahead, knowing I made a good decision. Neither the reader nor myself will know how it will eventually turn out. Disaster might strike, a building might collapse, a plane might not land or I could be hit by a bus on my way home. I am not sure that certainty is covered in the prediction.

A good behavioural therapist might be a better source of help by identifying reasons for a person's uncertainty about choices, pathways, jobs, or partners. Trusting your own decision might be the best fortunate outcome. If you allow a stranger to get involved with your future, you need to be aware of the implications. This person might gamble with your destiny. It would be better to put future luck in your own hands and make a dream a reality.

If you want to know if something could happen to you, the answer is always yes, it could. This statement encompasses the work of fortune-tellers and psychics – they work with possibilities.

Luck, animals and stones

I ask myself how a ladybug can make me luckier. Perhaps, if I believe it to be so, I would in a sense be more open to luck. They are certainly beautiful creatures and due to all the superstitions about them, they are called lucky ladybugs. Interestingly, luck is referred to as 'lady luck' and perhaps there is some significance in that. Again, I can refer to the 'psychology' of it – if you believe something to be so, it has some degree of meaning for you and you perceive it to be the truth. Ladybugs are shy insects and it is quite significant to feel one walking on your hand. If you wonder if you will be lucky as a result – only time will tell. Maybe it is just fiction made fact.

Some crystals do have healing powers and that is a fact, many healers and therapists use various crystals and stones in aromatherapy, reiki, massage therapy and general treatment of pain and discomfort. It is a fact that some crystals have the ability to draw out pain and to use them for healing would be considered a good-luck charm. The whole concept of finding special meaning in animals, stones, reptiles, and bugs just seem so farfetched for someone who views life realistically. Different cultures attach contradictory values to these external concepts and what is a cherished charm in one culture is considered a plague in another.

It makes sense that a lucky coin can bring you luck. Now and then, a unique coin becomes invaluable due to age and rarity and what was once a copper penny can suddenly be worth thousands of pounds. So, a coin may bring you unexpected luck if it is the right one.

I find it difficult to believe that a reptile such as a snake, iguana or lizard can bring me a pot of gold. Far better to go and find it at the end of the rainbow and not have a deadly venom injected into my blood stream as a consequence! The concept of luck in animals is definitely laden with superstition and I brush it off as superstition unique to the 'mind of the beholder'.

Free will versus determination

Logically, you cannot control the future. You will not consult a fortune teller to give you a specific or desired reading. It will be determined by 'how the chips will fall' on that particular day. If you have ever known someone who seems to consistently experience good luck, know this: they were born lucky.

Witches and fortune tellers – fact or fiction?

It was interesting to explore the subject of witches and fortune tellers throughout history. If I can make suppositions from everything I have read and transcribed, it would be a mixture of truth versus fiction: Witches do exist and witchcraft is still practised today. If you decide to get involved with either, it would be advisable to avail yourself of facts, warnings and risks. There are so many negative connotations associated with the two concepts that this in itself should be a warning for those who consider any possible association with witches or witchcraft.

Fortune telling is rife with controversy and many practices the art under false pretences. I hope the information provided will guide anyone who considers a psychic reading so that they can make an informed choice. I am not sure that witches or fortune tellers can bring any luck or fortune and the jury is certainly still out on that aspect.

People tend to search for happiness, love, luck and fortune in the wrong places. Sometimes all these riches are inside of us and with a little time, effort and patience we could be able to unearth these qualities without having to consult a witch, a seer or a reptile.

Chapter 5
Luck And Science

Luck And Science

The concept of luck has remained a mystery through the existence of mankind. Some people see it as the cause of one's success or downfall. It is a phenomenon that man has not been able to unravel or understand empirically. Many people will check their horoscopes or consult a spiritual counsellor to know if they should take a journey or proceed with certain actions. This book was written to shed some light on the mysterious phenomena of luck in a simple and concise manner so that when the reader is done, the concept of luck will be little clearer.

The largely dominant meritocratic paradigm of highly competitive Western cultures is rooted in the belief that success is mainly, if not exclusively, due to personal qualities such as talent, intelligence, skill, effort, wilfulness, resilience, hard work and risk-taking. Sometimes, we are willing to admit that a certain degree of luck could play a role in achieving success but it is rather common to underestimate the importance of external forces in individual success stories. It is very well known that intelligence (or talent and personal qualities) exhibits a Gaussian distribution among the population, whereas the distribution of wealth (often considered as a proxy of success) follows a typical power law (Pareto law) distribution, with the large majority of people being poor and a very small number of billionaires. Such a discrepancy between a normal distribution of inputs, with a typical scale (the average talent or intelligence), and the scale-invariant distribution of outputs, suggests that some hidden ingredient is at work here!

In 2018, Alessandro Pluchino, Alessio E. Biondo and Andrea Rapisarda, three researchers from the University of Catania in Italy proved, through a very interesting study titled 'Talent vs Luck: The role of Randomness in Success and Failure', that this hidden ingredient in explaining why someone is successful while another is not, is just randomness. In particular, their simple agent-based model shows that, if it is true that some degree of talent is necessary to be successful in life, then the most talented people almost never reach the highest peaks of success, often being overtaken by averagely talented but sensibly 'luckier' individuals. As far as we know, this counterintuitive result — although implicitly suggested between the lines in a vast amount of literature — is quantified in the study for the first time. It sheds new light on the effectiveness of assessing merit on the basis of a reached level of success and underlines the risks of distributing excessive honours or resources to people who, at the end of the day, could have simply been luckier than others.[1]

A ten-year scientific study into the nature of luck conducted by Richard Wiseman has revealed that, to a large extent, people make their own good and bad fortune. The results also show that it is possible to enhance the amount of luck that people encounter throughout their lives. *I personally don't agree with his conclusion, because conscious behaviour has nothing to do with luck. You consciously go and play the lottery, most people do, but most fail to win. Most people drive to work every day, few get killed by car accidents, while the majority survive the commute!*

The Luck Project

According to Richard Wiseman, superstition doesn't work because it is based on outdated and incorrect thinking. It comes from a time when people thought that luck was a strange force that could only be controlled by magical rituals and bizarre behaviours. Years ago, Mr. Wiseman decided to conduct a more scientific investigation into the concept of luck. He figured out that the best way to do this was to examine why some people are consistently lucky whilst others encounter little but ill-fortune. In short, why some people seem to live charmed lives full of lucky breaks and chance encounters, while others experience one disaster after another. He placed advertisements in national newspapers and magazines, asking for people who considered themselves exceptionally lucky or unlucky to contact him.

Over the years, 400 extraordinary men and women have volunteered to participate in his research; the youngest an eighteen-year-old student, the oldest an eighty-four-year-old retired accountant. Participants were drawn from all walks of life – businessmen, factory workers, teachers, housewives, doctors, secretaries, and salespeople. All were kind enough to let him put their lives and minds under the microscope. Jessica, a forty-two-year-old forensic scientist, was a typical lucky person in the group. She was in a long-term relationship with a man who she met completely by chance at a dinner party. In fact, good fortune has helped her achieve many of her lifelong ambitions. As she once explained to him, "I have my dream job, two wonderful children, and a great man that I love very much.

It's amazing, when I look back at my life, I realize that I have been lucky in just about every area." In contrast, the unlucky participants have not been so fortunate. Patricia, twenty-seven, has experienced bad luck throughout much of her life. A few years ago, she started to work as cabin crew for an airline and quickly gained a reputation as being accident-prone and a bad omen. One of her first flights had to make an unplanned stop-over because some passengers had become drunk and abusive. Another of Patricia's flights was struck by lightning, and just weeks later a third flight was forced to make an emergency landing.

Patricia was also convinced that her ill fortune could be transferred to others and so never wished people good luck because this had caused them to fail important interviews and exams. She is also unlucky in love and has moved from one broken relationship to the next. Patricia never seems to get any lucky breaks and always seems to be in the wrong place at the wrong time. Over the years that Mr. Wiseman interviewed these volunteers, he asked them to complete diaries, personality questionnaires, and intelligence tests and invited them to his laboratory to participate in experiments. His findings revealed that luck is not a magical ability or the result of random chance, nor are people born lucky or unlucky. Instead, although lucky and unlucky people have almost no insight into the real causes of their good and bad luck, their thoughts and behaviours are responsible for much of their fortune.

His research revealed that lucky people generate their own good fortune via four basic principles. They are skilled at creating and noticing chance opportunities, they make lucky decisions by listening to their intuition, they create self-fulfilling prophecies via positive expectations, and adopt a resilient attitude that transforms bad luck into good.[2]

Mr. Wiseman failed to explain why some people, who don't have the four basic principles of luck, would still win the lottery for example? Some lucky lottery winners were living miserable lives with a negative outlook for life and suddenly everything changed for them. I am sure so many of my readers do have and indeed apply these four principles in their lives, yet they don't advance much in life in terms of financial security, happiness, fulfilment and satisfaction, and they still feel unlucky!

I believe that what Mr. Wiseman thought were the four principles of a lucky life are actually the results of luck and not the cause for it. Luck came first, being born in one prosperous country and not poor one for example is luck coming 'first' to your life.

Luck and Counterfactual thinking

Janoff-Bulman[3] noted that victims of trauma and survivors of extreme negative events, such as rape, often react to these events by perceiving themselves as being lucky because they could imagine how their situation could have been worse. This kind of comparison between what has actually happened and what might have happened, but did not, has been termed 'counterfactual thinking'. A number of studies have empirically examined the role of counterfactual thinking in the attribution of an event to luck. In one study, Johnson (1986) had participants read descriptions of a day in the life of a college student that ended with either a major positive outcome, a major negative outcome, a major positive outcome that almost occurred but did not, or a major negative outcome that almost occurred. In a controlled scenario, no such major outcome was described as occurring or nearly occurring. Participants were asked to imagine themselves in the situation and to rate how lucky, happy and satisfied they would feel. 'Near losers' (i.e., those who nearly experienced a major negative event) were rated as luckier, but not necessarily happier and more satisfied, than those in the control condition, whilst 'near winners' (i.e., those who nearly experienced a major positive event) were regarded as less lucky than those in the control condition.

These findings suggest that the idea of what might have happened is an important factor in attributing an event to luck (or at least describing an event as lucky or unlucky). Note, however, that in this context the perception of luck is treated more as a subjective feeling rather than as a causal attribution. Nevertheless, the comparison to a counterfactual outcome appears to affect feelings of subjective luck and so, by association, luck may be perceived as a cause of the event (in that it was luck that prevented the counterfactual outcome from happening). Some recent work has further examined the role of counterfactual thinking in perceiving an event as lucky or unlucky. Teigen (1995) presented students with descriptions of lucky and unlucky events based on descriptions of incidents that had been provided by participants in a previous study. All explicit references to luck were removed and the students were asked to rate how attractive they considered each event, the degree to which they had the impression that something else could easily have happened, and how attractive this alternative would have been.

Unlucky events were generally rated as unattractive and as less attractive than lucky events, although lucky events were not rated as especially attractive in themselves. What seemed to be more important was that, for both types of events, participants had the impression that something else might have happened. That is, they were able to imagine counterfactual events that could have happened. Moreover, counterfactual comparisons associated with lucky events were regarded as less attractive than what actually happened, whilst for unlucky events, these counterfactuals were more attractive than the actual event. In a parallel study, in which students rated descriptions of positive and negative experiences, as opposed to lucky and unlucky experiences, counterfactual comparisons were not so easily imagined. This suggests that counterfactual thinking plays a role that is particular to perceiving an event as lucky or unlucky and it does not apply to positive or negative events as a whole.[4]

The Empirical Study of Luck

Almost everyone enjoys taking a risk every now and again[5] especially if the odds aren't too stacked against them and the loss penalty isn't too terrible. Some people believe that high-stakes in gambling is the answer to their desire for a thrill. The rapid transition from high nerve tension to the subsequent drop in tension seems to satisfy some primal craving connected with a sensation of danger. Others seemed to love endangering their own lives, and all too frequently the lives of others, as seen by the hundreds of people killed unnecessarily each year in car accidents. Whether we like it or not, everyone takes risks every day of their life. We must accept that taking chances is an unavoidable aspect of life. We live in a world of chance, and if we want to live sensibly, we must learn to take calculated risks. To do so, we must first learn and comprehend the rules of chance, which exist despite the fact that their presence is far from self-evident.

In a quest to comprehend the intricacies of the rules of chance, men were led to a succession of extraordinary ideas that we now refer to as superstitions. Some have persisted to this day, despite the fact that scientific results clearly contradict them. You may even occasionally come across someone who claims that he does not believe in science, but if you examine their behaviour closely, you will discover that they believe strongly in the rules of science, even if they are unaware of it. The notion of luck is one of the superstitious concepts that has survived through the ages. Chance occurrences, according to luck, do not occur randomly. They are controlled by a mysterious force known as luck, which is tied to every man like his shadow, except that the latter may be sent away by walking into darkness, whilst the former will follow him everywhere.

The Belief in Good Luck Scale

According to an article entitled, The Belief in Good Luck Scale by Peter R. Darke and Jonathan L. Freedman [6], Three studies have shown that reliable individual variations exist when it comes to belief in luck. Some people have an unreasonable conviction that chance is a somewhat steady factor that tends to affect events in their favour, while others appear to believe that chance is unpredictable and unreliable. Furthermore, these views exhibited a high level of consistency throughout time. The Belief in Good Luck was linked to locus of control (mostly through a chance subscale).

General optimism, academic pessimism, self-esteem, the need for control, and success drive were not linked to belief in good luck. There was also evidence that believing in good fortune was separate from feeling lucky or content with one's life. The Belief in Good Luck scale also revealed ethnic group disparities, with Asian-Americans being more prone to believe in superstitions about luck than non-Asians. Finally, the Belief in Good Luck scale was proven to predict favourable outcomes for common events that are generally linked with luck. This is consistent with prior research demonstrating that people who believe in personal good fortune react to happy events by becoming more optimistic about the chances of future good fortune.

Traditional views on the conditions commonly connected with expectations for success and luck include perceptions of luck (e.g., Rotter, 1966; Kelley, 1967; Weineret al., 1972). These theories, in general, imply that luck is a random, uncontrolled force that has minimal bearing on future predictions. Although this is scientifically valid, many individuals appear to perceive luck in a way that contradicts this viewpoint. The goal of the experiments presented in these studies was to construct a reliable measure of irrational beliefs about luck and then investigate some of the consequences of these beliefs on success expectations. Rotter's social learning theory of personality (1955, 1966) was one of the first to uncover elements that contribute to control perceptions.[7]

Control should increase when events are perceived to be largely determined by an individual's own activities (internal locus of control), but decrease if events appear to be caused by luck or other people (external locus of control). On the basis of their reinforcement history in other circumstances, individuals may acquire generalized expectations of control.

Perceived control might thus be drawn either directly from previous experience in the same environment or more broadly from dispositional beliefs of one's capacity to influence events. In either situation, perceived control should be reduced to a level at which luck is thought to have played a role. It appeared that some people "believe in luck", which means that they feel that good luck regularly leads to success in their everyday lives. People may state that they have lucky days or that they consider themselves to be fortunate in general. These remarks seem to show that luck is seen as a personal trait that is at least partly consistent throughout time. To put it another way, rather than holding on to the reasonable belief that luck is external and unstable, at least some individuals talk about good luck as if it were the polar opposite - personal and stable.[8]

Role of chance/luck in scientific discoveries

The role of chance, or "luck", in science comprises all the ways in which unexpected discoveries are made. The field of

Psychology, especially, is concerned with the way science interacts with chance - particularly how "serendipity" (accidents that, through sagacity, are transformed into opportunity) affects science. Psychologist Kevin Dunbar and colleagues estimate that between 30% and 50% of all scientific discoveries are accidental in some sense (see examples below)[9]

Psychologist Alan A. Baumeister says a scientist must be "sagacious" (attentive and clever) to benefit from an accident.[10]

Dunbar quotes Louis Pasteur's saying that "Chance favours only the prepared mind". The prepared mind, Dunbar suggests, is one trained for observational rigour. Dunbar adds that there is a great deal of writing about the role that serendipity ("happy accidents") plays in the scientific method.

Serendipitous Discoveries

Royston Roberts says that various discoveries required a degree of genius, but also some lucky element for that genius to act on.[11]

Richard Gaughan writes that accidental discoveries result from the convergence of preparation, opportunity, and desire.[12]

An example of luck in science is when drugs under investigation become known for treating different, unexpected diseases. This was the case for minoxidil (an antihypertensive vasodilator that was subsequently found to also slow hair loss and promote hair regrowth in some people) and for sildenafil (a medicine for pulmonary arterial hypertension, now familiar as "Viagra", used to treat erectile dysfunction). The hallucinogenic effects of lysergic acid diethylamide (LSD) were discovered by Albert Hofmann, who was originally working to try and treat migraines and bleeding after childbirth. Hofmann experienced mental distortions and suspected it may have been the effects of LSD. He decided to test this hypothesis on himself by taking what he thought was "an extremely small quantity" or 250 micrograms of LSD. (For comparison, a typical dose of LSD for recreational use in the modern day is 50 micrograms). Hofmann's description of what he experienced as a result of taking so much LSD is regarded by Royston Roberts as "one of the most frightening accounts in recorded medical history".

Different understandings of luck

Luck is interpreted and understood in many different ways.[13]

Luck as lack of control

Luck refers to the things that happen beyond a person's control. This view incorporates phenomena that are chance happenings such as a person's place of birth for example, but where there is no uncertainty involved, or where the uncertainty is irrelevant. Within this framework, one can differentiate between three different types of luck:

Constitutional luck, that is, luck with factors that cannot be changed. Place of birth and genetic constitution are typical examples. Circumstantial luck, with factors that are haphazardly brought on such as accidents and epidemics.

Ignorance luck, that is, luck with factors one does not know about. Examples can be identified only in hindsight.

Serendipitous luck, which is circumstantial luck pertaining to favourable discoveries and/or inventions.

Luck as a fallacy

Another view holds that "luck is probability taken personally". A rationalist approach to luck includes the application of the rules of probability and an avoidance of unscientific beliefs. The rationalist thinks that the belief in luck is a result of poor reasoning or wishful thinking. To a rationalist, a believer in luck who asserts that something has influenced his or her luck commits the "post hoc ergo propter hoc" logical fallacy: that because two events are connected sequentially, they are connected causally as well.

So, in general: A happens (luck-attracting event or action) and then B happens; therefore, A influenced B.

More contemporary authors writing on the subject believe that the definition of good destiny is: One who enjoys good health; has the physical and mental capabilities to achieve his goals in life; has a good appearance; has happiness in mind and is not prone to accidents.[14] In the rationalist perspective, probability is only affected by confirmed causal connections.

The gambler's fallacy and inverse gambler's fallacy both explain some reasoning problems in common beliefs in luck. It involves denying the unpredictability of random events: "I haven't rolled a seven all week, so I'll definitely roll one tonight". Philosopher Daniel Dennett wrote that "luck is mere luck" rather than a property of a person or thing.

Luck as an essence

There is also a series of spiritual, or supernatural beliefs regarding fortune. These beliefs vary widely, but most agree that luck can be influenced through spiritual means by performing certain rituals or by avoiding certain circumstances. Luck can also be a belief in an organization of fortunate and unfortunate events. Here, luck is a form of superstition which is interpreted differently by different individuals. Carl Jung coined the term synchronicity, which he described as "a meaningful coincidence". Many traditional African practices, such as voodoo and hoodoo, have a strong belief in superstition. Some of these religions include a belief that third parties can influence an individual's luck. Shamans and witches are both respected and feared, based on their ability to cause good or bad fortune for those in villages near them.

Luck as a self-fulfilling prophecy

Some evidence supports the idea that belief in luck acts like a placebo, producing positive thinking and improving people's responses to events. In personality psychology, people reliably differ from each other depending on four key aspects: beliefs in luck, rejection of luck, being lucky, and being unlucky.[15] People who believe in good luck are more optimistic, more satisfied with their lives, and have better moods. People who believe they are personally unlucky experience more anxiety and is less likely to take advantage of unexpected opportunities. One 2010 study found that golfers who were told they were using a "lucky ball" performed better than those who were not.[16]

Are the most successful people in society simply the luckiest people?

Professor Scott Barry Kaufman spent his entire career studying the psychological characteristics that predict achievement and success. While he has found that a certain number of traits including passion, perseverance, imagination, intellectual curiosity, and openness to experience do significantly explain differences in success, he was often intrigued by how much of the variance was often left unexplained. In recent years, a number of studies and books, including those by risk analyst Nassim Taleb, investment strategist Michael Mauboussin, and economist Robert Frank, have suggested that luck and opportunity may play a far greater role across a number of fields, including financial trading, business, sports, art, music, literature, and science, than we ever realised.

Their argument is not that luck is everything of course, talent matters. Instead, the data suggests that we miss out on a really importance piece of the success picture if we only focus on personal characteristics in attempting to understand the determinants of success.[17] In short, these studies concluded that luck and opportunity play an underappreciated role in determining the final level of individual success.

Science did prove the existence of luck, scientists were able to determine the existence of a random force that affects people's lives regardless of their education, hard work, ethnicity, persistence...etc, but science still failed to explain the mechanism of luck, its dynamics, its components and its laws. Just like the many unexplained mysteries and events in our world, luck remains an elusive force, we can sense its existence in our lives, but we cannot control it like we control some other forces like wind or solar power, we cannot initiate it like we initiate light.

It makes me wonder whether luck belongs to the paranormal world, a world completely beyond the reach of science!

Chapter 6

The Lucky Mentality

The Lucky Mentality

In this chapter, I am presenting the school of thought that sees luck as something you can attract to your life, at least to some extent. Although some techniques can help, I still strongly believe that luck can't be controlled or even harnessed. A person who wins millions of pounds in the lottery did not do anything that the millions of people who lost in the same lottery did not! They all did the same thing - buying the ticket. Only one won, while millions lost. The question remains: Why? Why that person specifically?

Let us go through the thoughts and ideas that emphasise personal choice and control over luck and examine them in detail. The idea of luck has long been debated. Is it something you invite into your life? Are some people just born lucky? Or, is it something you create through the way you think?

Despite an abundance of mystical theories, the likelihood is that luck is something we bring into our own lives. The way we think affects the way we act. The right mentality allows us to spot opportunities and take them. That, in itself, can appear like a bolt of luck, like being in the right place at the right time. In reality, having the right mindset breathes energy into your life.

In effect, you make your own luck. So, how can you develop this 'lucky mentality'?

Is luck a state of mind?

There is no doubt that luck exists. However, the advocates of a lucky mentality believe that it is very unlikely to be something that is decided by a higher mystical power. It has far more to do with your attitude and mentality. Look at it this way - when a new opportunity comes your way, are you likely to take it? That depends upon how you are feeling on that given day. If you are feeling positive, upbeat, and happy, you are more likely to see that opportunity in a positive light. You will be curious, and keen to see where it leads. Of course, that means you will take the opportunity. However, if you are feeling down and negative, assuming that everything will go wrong, you will pass over that opportunity.

Countless studies have attempted to work out whether or not luck is a mysterious occurrence or something we control ourselves. It is nice to think that someone bestows a good fortune upon us because they feel like doing so, but it is far more likely that luck is indeed a state of mind. This is great news though because it means you can bring more luck into your life by changing your mentality. The other plus point is that by developing that lucky mentality, you will naturally become a more positive person.

Considering this - how do you explain lottery wins? You cannot control which numbers come up on the lottery, and that's where the grey area begins!

Life throws us chance occurrences now and again. For instance, it is wonderful to believe that there is some kind of magical interference going on when a poor couple win the lottery and suddenly become millionaires. We romanticize it because the story is heart-warming. It makes us think that perhaps that sort of thing can happen to us too. However, the decision to play the lottery that night was personal, and if they chose differently, they would not have won. Again, perhaps it comes down to that "maybe it will work out" mentality.

Luck is something you can create for yourself to a certain degree, but there will always be times when unexplained things happen. Because we cannot explain them, we put them down to something mystical that we cannot see, and in most cases, that is luck.

The truth is that as humans we like to be able to measure things. We do not trust things that are invisible to us because that means they are not measurable and cannot be proven. We are extremely sceptical of anything that does not allow us to study it, which is why the idea of luck has long been debated.

You cannot see luck, you cannot feel it, you cannot measure it, and you cannot predict it. However, one thing all scientists agree on is that you can indeed create your own luck by changing your mentality and becoming a more positive person. That might not explain every single lucky event that happens in life, but it goes a long way towards shedding some light on it. We have all heard the story of someone who had a very close brush with death. Perhaps they were driving a car and they missed a collision by a split second. We say "it must have been their lucky day", after all, had they set off on their journey a second later, they would have been right in the middle of that collision.

Where luck is concerned, some things cannot be explained, but isn't that what makes it so wonderful? Perhaps we need to focus more on the things we can control and resort to appreciating the things that we cannot. Chance events happen all the time simply because of the decisions we make. A need to control everything will result in a rigid life that resists the influx of new energy. Luck is very unlikely to come your way when you have a rigid mindset because you will never take a chance. When you take small, measured risks, you are far more likely to notice the good things coming your way. At the end of the day, isn't that what luck is all about?

Do lucky people have a specific mentality?

Advocates of the 'Lucky Mentality' believe that nobody is born lucky or unlucky. You can read into superstitions all day long, but if you break a mirror, you will just have a broken mirror to clean up - not seven years of bad luck. (However, cleaning up a broken mirror is no fun and could lead to a cut or two, which may just be your bad luck!) If you have a more open-minded, positive, and upbeat approach to life, you are more likely to spot opportunities that could be considered lucky. In that case, there is no such thing as a lucky person but simply someone who has a more positive approach to life.

Positive thinking and all its benefits are something we are going to explore in more detail later on in this chapter. On the flip side, stress, anxiety and depression are running riot these days. According to the World Health Organization[1], around 264 million people suffer from depression worldwide. Being depressed, whether it is short-lived or long-term, makes people negative and does not allow you to see opportunities as positive events that could occur in your life.

Perhaps the 'lucky mentality' we are all so keen to develop is more about being happy than anything else. Without being insensitive to the severe and devastating effects of clinical depression, but have you ever heard of a lucky depressed person? No. That is because luck is something you create yourself. We have already explored that there are chance occurrences in life that cannot be explained but those are out of our control. The things you can control come down to how you think because it controls how you act.

Let us look at an example of a person with an upbeat mentality versus someone with a more downcast, perhaps depressed mentality.

Scenario:

A person sees an advertisement for a vacation whilst browsing social media. The advertisement promises blue seas, white sands, endless sun, and a great social setting in an all-inclusive hotel. The price is cut for a set amount of time.

Positive person - This person sees the advertisement and is immediately swept away by the beautiful images of the ocean and the sun. They read the text and there is a small voice in their head that says "that looks wonderful, maybe I should go". They don't jump into action straight away, but instead, they read a bit more and then go on to read the comments. They go about their day but the image of that blue sea just won't leave their mind. When they return home, they decide to call the number and find out a little more. Once they have the information they need, they decide that they are going to go. The price is low, they have the time off work, and it might be a great opportunity to kick back and relax.

Negative person - This person sees the advertisement and enjoys the images. Rather than being swept away by the romance of it all, they feel sad that they will never get to see somewhere as beautiful as that. They immediately assume they can't afford it, without even looking at the price. They assume that they will probably get homesick and wish they had never gone. They look at the images a little more, before continuing to scroll through their social media feed. They don't give it another thought.

How can this turn into luck?

The negative person has already thrown out the idea, without it becoming even a possibility. They just assumed that it wasn't for them and carried on with their day. However, the positive person stayed open-minded to the idea of the vacation and did some extra research to find out the details. Once they had those details, they made a decision based on whether they could afford it and whether they would enjoy it.

The negative person doesn't go on vacation. However, the positive person does, and during that vacation, they meet other travellers with the same mindset. They end up having a wonderful time and make some new friends, some of which end up as life-long friends. These new friends may live in different countries, which could lead to new travel opportunities. Some of these new friends may even be business opportunities that could benefit the positive person financially.

Can you see how making one decision with an open mind can lead to a chain reaction of new possibilities? These possibilities could easily be classed as lucky but they come down to making one positive decision and seeing where it leads.

Luck is about being open to new things. It is that simple. The lucky mentality is therefore nothing more than a positive attitude to life, being open-minded, willing to take well-researched, measured risks and having a "who knows where this will lead" mindset.

The difficulty in explaining the lucky mentality lies in the types of examples we discussed before - chance occurrences or narrow escapes. According to the lucky mentality advocates, these aren't actually down to luck, they are just a series of decisions or events that build up to a crescendo. There is no higher power dictating the lottery numbers that fall out of the machine - it's a random event and someone has to win. The decision to play the lottery is all it takes and the rest is literally up to chance! This does however not explain why Jack specifically wins the lottery while Steven and millions of others lose?

Narrow escapes also come down to a series of smaller decisions and events that lead to a final result. You left home five minutes later because you could not get out of bed. Do you believe that is luck trying to save you from a terrible fate, or simply that you liked the feel of your bed and wanted an extra five minutes? Yes, you can look back on it and thank your metaphorical lucky stars, but is it just that you made a decision at that moment and that is where it led you?

You can sit and tie yourself up in knots trying to prove luck one way or another but according to the believers in the lucky mentality, countless 'studies' have all confirmed that we do indeed make our own luck to a huge degree. Chance things will always happen because that is life, and in many ways, that is what makes it so wonderful and unpredictable. Let us be honest, if we could predict everything that was going to happen, it would be very boring indeed, wouldn't it?

What does a lucky mentality look like?

So, what leads a 'lucky' person to think and feel the way they do? Can it be changed and adjusted, or are you stuck with the same mentality you developed throughout your life?

To explore what the lucky mentality looks like, we need to think about a few separate subjects starting with superstition, then serendipity, luck in retrospect and seizing future opportunities.

Superstition

A person deemed to be "lucky" may just be quite superstitious. They believe that if they open their umbrella indoors, they are due to bad luck, or if they accidentally cross two knives at the dinner table, something bad is going to happen. However, they also believe that superstition can bring good luck, such as saluting at magpies or finding a feather.

Superstition isn't a bad thing but the problem comes in when someone ends up being so obsessed by superstition that it turns into anxiety. Mirrors break, sometimes by total accident, but a severely superstitious person could become stressed about the chances of bringing negative luck into their lives and therefore change their actions to become more reserved or careful. A so-called "lucky person" may also be slightly superstitious, but end up taking everything with a pinch of salt. When they see a good luck sign, they may use that to push them towards making decisions that could turn into possibilities. This is an example of when superstition becomes a positive influence, thereby improving a person life.

Serendipity

Serendipity is chance events with positive outcomes. For instance, you could say that meeting the love of your life was serendipitous because of a chain of events that led up to that meeting. You could say that it was fate, or you could simply say that it was a series of decisions made by both of you that lead you to that point in life.

It is entirely impossible to prove whether serendipity exists or not. We can't see it or measure it, and as already mentioned, humans are extremely sceptical of anything that cannot be measured. However, we love the idea of something that seems romantic and mystical, which is why the words 'fate', 'destiny', and 'serendipity' came to exist.

Whether it truly exists or not, a person with a lucky mentality is more likely to welcome it into their lives and encourage more of it, simply by their actions and mindset. You will see acts that you could deem to be serendipitous every single day if you look hard enough. You took the wrong turning at the junction and ended up driving a different way to work. That made you a few minutes late and as a result, you ended up talking to a new person in the elevator. You end up marrying that person you met in the elevator. Is it fate or destiny, or just a series of events? That is a true example of serendipity but a person with a lucky mentality accepts these so-called bumps as new opportunities, focussing on the positive.

If you were downcast and negative, you would probably get angry about your accidental detour. You may be so annoyed at yourself that you barely even speak to the person in the elevator. They may get the wrong impression of you and you may never meet again. It is not chance, it's about your mentality and your resulting actions.

In truth, serendipity is just the willingness to try new things every day, mix up your schedule and accept any obstacles that come your way. Trust that whatever happens will turn out fine, and by doing all of that, you are opening yourself up to meeting new people and having new experiences. All of this brings a wealth of opportunities your way, which could easily be put down to serendipity.

Luck in Retrospect

It is easy to see luck in retrospect. For instance, you can look back on an event and think "Wow, that was lucky" when in truth, you just made good decisions to get you there. You may not have known they were good decisions at the time, but you did what you felt was right and the result was good. This is part of the lucky mentality.

To look back and identify retrospective luck, the outcome of the event had to be favourable to you. Of course, there are always going to be times when the event doesn't fall in your favour and instead, favours someone else. It doesn't mean that your luck wasn't in that day, it means that they made better decisions or that it was just a chance occurrence.

We can all sit down and think about retrospective luck and come up with series of events that turned out well for us. Maybe you won a competition, met someone new and exciting in a cafe, or you received the promotion you worked so hard for. We deem those events to be lucky because they turned out well for us, however, there is always someone in that same situation who it turned out badly for, or who chance just didn't favour at that time.

A person with a lucky mentality is, therefore, able to influence their own luck by not only making the best choices for them at the time but by also working hard for the things that will bring good fortune their way. If you gain a promotion at work, you weren't lucky, you most likely worked hard!

Taking responsibly for the things that happen in your life, ironically, brings more luck your way. Sitting around expecting things to fall into your lap isn't going to make good things happen. A person with a downcast attitude will simply allow one small failure to stop them from trying anything else in the future. However, a person with a positive attitude, and therefore a 'lucky mentality', will learn from the mistakes of that failure and make sure they do better next time. Therefore, in effect, they're making their own luck.

Seizing future opportunities

A person with a lucky mentality can carve out opportunities for themselves and take the ones that are presented to them. That is the simplest way to bring more luck into your life. You can't tell at any given moment whether an opportunity given to you will turn out to be a positive thing or not. What you need is the willingness to take measured risks to find out.

That doesn't mean grabbing every single chance that comes your way and blindly throwing yourself into it. It means thinking for a while before choosing the opportunities that you think are going to bring you what you want, or the ones that simply seem like fun and could turn out to be great additions to your life. Lucky mentality people don't necessarily take every chance that comes their way but they're open-minded to where something could lead and choose their opportunities wisely.

Luck can be carved out of anything. You could end up in a situation that seems negative to begin with, but the choices you make afterwards turn it into something much more positive. For example, you could stall your car at a crossing and the person behind you accidentally runs into the back of you. That is not a particularly positive situation, but you may strike up a conversation with that person and they could end up being a great new friend, or maybe even the love of your life. You could argue serendipity, or you could say that it's just about having the right attitude.

With a negative attitude, you may shout and berate that person, refusing to accept responsibility for your part in the accident. While, with a positive attitude, you could see both sides, apologize for your stalling your car, and agree to work through the issue together. Again, it comes down to attitude and mentality and not a mystical power throwing two people together. Recognising the different ways that luck can be perceived gives you a very clear glimpse into what a lucky mentality looks like. A person with a lucky mentality may be aware that they're trying to bring luck into their life or they may simply be open to opportunities.

What can you do to help boost the amount of luck in your life, via the way you think, act, and feel? Can you train yourself to develop a lucky mentality? Everyone wants to encourage more positive events into their life, whether they call it luck or not. While nobody is born lucky or unlucky, many people do develop a positive and open-minded mentality very early on in their lives. This boosts their chances of creating and taking opportunities throughout their life, making them appear luckier than someone who doesn't have this way of thinking.

The good news? You can change your mentality and mindset at any time. It takes time and effort and it is not going to happen overnight, but it is entirely possible to rewire your brain to think in a more positive way.

There are a few tools you can use to help develop this new, lucky mentality. For example, learning to trust your intuition and allowing it to guide you, positive thinking, forcing yourself to try new things, being open-minded as opposed to closed-minded, try to maximize the opportunities that come your way and finally repetition to rewire the brain.

Trust Your Intuition as a Guide

Whether you believe that your intuition is some spooky sixth sense or you see it as a gut feeling that can be used to guide you throughout your life, is neither here nor there. The fact is that intuition is a very strong tool you can use and it has been proven to exist[2]. Again, we are sceptical of the things we can't see with our own eyes or measure with a set of scales or a ruler, but in this case, you are just going to have to go with blind hope!

To develop your new lucky mentality, intuition can be used to help you pick the right opportunities to pursue, versus the ones you can allow to pass you by. Remember, so-called lucky people don't just go with whatever opportunity comes their way, they are just as picky as you! The difference is that they see things a little differently and give themselves time to picture how it might turn out, with a more positive spin. This informs their choice of whether to go with it or not.

Unfortunately, learning to trust your intuition can take time if you have never really paid it much attention before. It is a little like a muscle you work out at the gym - you need to flex it regularly, over a long period of time, to make it stronger. You also need to boost your belief in it, especially if you are unsure whether it is going to work for you.

The answer? Try it and go with it – it is as simple as that. Start small and move to bigger, more important decisions. They call it your 'gut feeling' for a reason. Your intuition isn't situated in any particular place within your body but most people tend to feel a specific sensation in their gut. It might be butterflies, it might be a sense of doom, it might be a feeling of nausea and it is usually different for everyone. That means you need to learn how to tune into your intuition, for you and you alone.

Gut feeling exercise!

The next time an opportunity comes your way, acknowledge it as something you can choose to go with or ignore. Tell yourself that there may be positives in this and that you need to assess them before throwing the idea out. Sit down somewhere comfortably and close your eyes, turn your attention to your breath and slow your breathing down - breathe in through your nose for a slow count of five, and then exhale slowly through your mouth for another count of five. Repeat this until you feel calmer – it is not easy to try and work out how you feel about something when your mind is whirring!

When you are ready, focus on the opportunity and be mindful of how you feel about it when you picture it in your mind. Do you feel excited? Do you feel fearful? Do you feel very unsure? Do you feel angry? Try and label what you are feeling.

Visualize the opportunity and explore your inner feelings as you do so. You may find that you hear something in your mind, perhaps even a voice telling you what to do. This may sound a little 'out there' for the first-time user, but it is simply your intuition trying to guide you towards something which could be beneficial for you, or warning you to avoid something because it is probably not going to work out how you want it to.

You can choose to listen to your intuition or ignore it. It is not fool proof; however, it is a good guide to help you when you're not sure which way to turn.

The first time you try to use your intuition you may find that you don't feel anything. That is fine, it can take time to build up your intuition and your sense of belief in it too. Keep trying and stick with it. The more you use your intuition, the stronger it will become and the more you can rely upon it to help you out during times when you are 'umming' and 'ahhing' between two choices.

Do so-called lucky people use their intuition knowingly? Some do but others tend to go with their gut without really understanding why. Again, some people are just naturally more intuitive than others and they don't necessarily need to build up their belief in their intuition. However, if you need to do so, start now and stick with it. It is something you can use to guide you throughout your life in many different ways.

Positive Thinking

Learning to be more positive in general can have a huge effect on your life. It can also help you to create and maintain that lucky mentality that you desire. So-called lucky people are upbeat and more positive than those who deem themselves to be unlucky. Someone who sees everything in a negative light is just going to allow opportunities to pass them by because they assume it is not going to work out. It is Tigger versus Eeyore (from Winnie the Pooh). Tigger is full of energy, bounding around everywhere, and trying new things. He doesn't mind talking to new people and he just wants to have fun and enjoy himself. On the other hand, Eeyore is very self-doubting. He prefers to stay firmly within his comfort zone, fearful of anything unknown. Whilst you don't have to have the unwavering energy of Tigger (that would be nothing short of exhausting), you do need to follow his example in becoming a more positive person.

The truth is that when you are more upbeat about life, you see things differently. Everything is brighter and more hopeful. However, when you see everything negatively, you are fearful without even realizing it. You see everything as likely to fail. You assume that trying new things will just be too much trouble and cause too much stress. You worry about what other people are going to think if it doesn't work out, and you end up tying yourself up in knots. Positive people still have these thoughts to some degree, but they can set them aside and allow positivity to triumph. Not everything you attempt in life is going to work out. Sometimes you will find that you end up hitting a dead end and you wonder where you can go from there. You can stop, take note and learn from your choices saying, "Okay, that didn't work, now onto the next thing!" A positive person is far more likely to take it on the chin and accept that it didn't work out, compared to a negative person who is just going to dwell on what they perceive to be a failure. Dwelling on failure isn't going to encourage new opportunities into your life, because you will be unwilling to try something new. In that case, luck isn't going to come your way.

A negative person also spends a huge amount of time worrying about what other people think. A positive person thinks about it but decides not to care so much. It's not an easy point to get to, especially if you lack self-confidence, but working on it will benefit you in many ways.

Forcing Yourself to Try New Things

You know the saying, "when one door closes, another opens". There is a lot of truth in the saying in terms of forcing yourself to try new things. You are opening new doors and bringing fresh opportunities into your life. When you do that, the chance of a so-called lucky occurrence increases. You never know what could come of taking a different route to work or going for a walk in a different part of town. These are small, almost inconsequential things, but who knows who you could meet or what you could see.

If you stay in your comfort zone and don't try anything new, you are not going to see much new energy coming your way. Sure, you might notice the odd so-called lucky event, probably out of pure chance, but in terms of noticing major changes? Not so likely. Instead, you are likely to become more negative about the fact that you don't seem to be moving anywhere and you could become sceptic about the whole idea of luck and happiness in general.

If you are not someone who finds it easy to push themselves beyond their comfort zone, take baby steps. Don't try and run before you can walk and just see where that takes you. Once you start to see that nothing terrible happens when you try new things, you will be keen to keep going and try more. If something doesn't work out, don't beat yourself up about it, instead, be happy about the fact that you tried.

For instance, if you don't tend to go out on your own and you always wait for someone to invite you out, try going to the cinema alone. That is a far easier step than going out to dinner on your own and although it may bring fewer opportunities your way, it does boost your confidence to take a bigger step next time.

The same goes for work opportunities - maybe you see an advert for a job that you would love to do but you are pretty sure you don't have enough experience. You can either just look at the advert wistfully or wish that things were different before carrying on with your day, or you can put in an application anyway. You can look for transferrable skills that can fill the gaps in places you lack experience and make a point of mentioning how passionate you are about the role – convince them you are the best candidate for the job. You may get it, you may not, but at least you tried and you don't have that "what if" hanging over your head. By applying, you at least stand a chance of getting an interview. Then you have another opportunity before you, a chance to impress the panel and go on to get the job, something you were pretty sure you had no realistic shot at. In life, we make our own magic. We have to get up each morning and do something to kickstart a chain of events that take us towards what we want. If we don't do anything and refuse to try new things, the same old routine will just keep repeating itself. Isn't life a little too short for that? By forcing yourself to try new things you are increasing the chances of being in the right place at the right time, of meeting new people, and of an exciting opportunity coming your way.

Try going to work differently, perhaps walking or cycling, or trying a different route. Go to another cafe for your morning coffee, or try a new restaurant that's recently opened in town. These are all small changes that could increase your chances of bringing more luck into your life. It doesn't have to be something huge, small things can increase your confidence and encourage you to go after bigger things in the future.

Being more open-minded

If you are not someone who is generally very open-minded, it can be difficult to encourage yourself to change the way you think. However, it is entirely possible. Becoming a more open-minded person will benefit you hugely and it is never going to be a waste of effort. Being open-minded means being able to acknowledge other's viewpoints and accepting other people's opinions as being just as valid as yours. It means accepting everyone as they are too. None of this is a bad thing, and it can help you reach out and meet people from all different walks of life. Being open-minded can enrich your life.

Research has shown[3] that there are several ways you can encourage yourself to be more open-minded. These all involve getting out of your comfort zone and challenging yourself to think in different ways. Again, it is not easy but it's something you can work towards over some time. A good option is to sit down and have a good-natured debate with a friend about something that has several different sides. Choose a subject that you potentially disagree on and then talk about it. Do your best to see their side and to ask useful questions that help you to understand their point of view. Rather than shutting them down and insisting that your side is right, listen to what they have to say. Then, after the debate, write down a list of points supporting each side of the argument. Write down your side and then write down theirs. Look back over their side and see if there is any common ground you can agree on. This particular exercise helps you to get some perspective and is a useful enlightening tool.

It is also useful to try and challenge your thinking in everyday life. Ask yourself why you believe a certain thing to be true. What made you think that way and what proved it to you? Why do you think other people think differently? Where is the grey area and why does it exist? Could it be that you are both right and that it is just a matter of opinion? To be open-minded you need to challenge your long-held beliefs to understand that there are two sides to every story. Sometimes there are more than two sides!

Learning to be more open-minded is something you need to practice. It is not necessarily about being more tolerant because many people are very tolerant but aren't necessarily open-minded in terms of the decisions they make. It is more about being able to look at a situation and see that there are several different potential outcomes, depending upon the action you take. When you think that way, you start to develop an "anything is possible" mindset.

Capture opportunities and maximize them

It is not just about seizing opportunities, but also about being able to maximize their potential at the same time. For instance, you could do well in a job interview and decide that you are going to take the job. That is indeed capturing an opportunity. Now, you can either just go to work do what you have to do and then go home, or you can do a little more. Become part of the team, work hard, volunteer for side projects and go the extra mile. That means you are maximizing the opportunity and potentially creating even more opportunities as a result.

It is not good enough just to grab an opportunity and rest on your laurels; if you want to keep breathing new energy into your life, you have to continue to strive to be better and push yourself to keep achieving. Luck doesn't fall into your lap; it is something that is achieved through hard work and taking chances when they come your way. The next time an opportunity presents itself, ask yourself what you can do to take even more advantage of it. Write a list and aim to keep working hard to milk that opportunity for all its worth. Ask yourself what else may come of it and allow yourself to push the boundaries of chance. A positive, go-getter mindset, a good opportunity and a lot of hard work can achieve almost anything!

Use Repetition as a Learning Tool

Many studies have shown that the brain learns by repetition[4]. When you were in school and you were learning the alphabet, can you remember your teacher getting the class to sing the alphabet song over and over again? It probably drove your Parents crazy at the time but you kept singing it because it was stuck in your head. Did you ever forget the alphabet? No! The same goes for numbers. We are taught to count from 1 to 10 over and over again, to memorize the numbers in the correct sequence, because the brain learns via repetition.

The more you repeat something, the more your brain believes it to be true. That is why positive affirmations are so effective - more on those a little later! When you repeat something, it is stored in the hippocampus[5], effectively the memory store of your brain. This means that when you want to recall that information, it's easily pulled to the front of your mind and you can remember it. If you want to become a so-called luckier person and develop the mentality that most lucky people have, you need to use the power of repetition to change your mindset. Tell yourself regularly that you are a lucky person[6]. Those who believe themselves to be lucky, are generally luckier, not because there is some mystical work at hand. People who think positively and believe that luck is coming their way, are simply more likely to notice opportunities.

The more you repeat these positive affirmations, the more you are rewiring your brain into becoming a person with a lucky mentality. Tell yourself that new opportunities could bring wonderful energy into your life, and you will believe it. Then, tell yourself that today could be the day you change your life, and you will have more hope. The brain is a very sophisticated organ, but it can be tricked very easily when you know how to do it!

These few tricks will help you to develop a lucky mentality but remember that nothing is going to change overnight. Don't become discouraged if you don't see instant changes because you are rewiring your brain here! All of these things take time. The good news is that after a short amount of time has passed, you will be able to see the difference in how you feel and how you act. The truth is that your emotions do affect your actions[7]. So, by changing your emotions via the way you think, you can change your actions too. That could lead you to seize more opportunities, creating new ones, and changing your life for the better. In this case, it's not a mystical force at play, but you creating your very own source of luck.

How can positive thinking help with developing a lucky mentality?

Another useful tactic in developing a lucky mentality is positive thinking. There are major plus points to becoming a more positive person but the truth is that humans are born with negative as their default setting. The reason for this is because our brains like to protect us from potential threats. As a result, thinking negatively helps you to stay safe and stops you from taking unnecessary chances that could lead you toward danger. On the other hand, taking unnecessary chances could be defined as taking an opportunity that comes your way. That is exactly what you need to do to become luckier! It stands to reason that by thinking more positively, you could increase your good fortune and be happier and healthier in the process.

Positive thinking isn't just about creating opportunities, it has many other benefits too. There are some very strong health benefits to positive thinking[8], including a longer life due to reduced stress and better heart health, less chance of depression and anxiety, lower stress levels, boosted immune system (particularly against the common cold), the ability to cope better with stress and increased quality of relationships. These are all benefits that positive thinking can bring into your life but besides that – it feels so much better to be a Tigger than an Eeyore? And, don't you find that people would rather be around those who are upbeat compared to those who always see the glass as half empty?

If being more positive can bring more self-harvested luck into your life and make you happier and healthier at the same

165

time, it is an endeavour you should be spending your time on. So, how can you become a more positive person? Let us look at a few techniques you can try, but again, it is important to remember that it is not going to happen overnight. Don't start with your new positive mindset and then feel downcast the next day when you have negative thoughts. It is going to take time to get used to, but then you will start to see the positive effects coming your way. Before you can begin to become more positive, you first need to learn to be mindful of your thoughts so you can identify a negative thought coming your way. This can be quite exhausting at first because a lot of the time we think without even being aware of it. However, turning your attention inwards and labelling a thought as positive or negative will help you to identify where work needs to be done.

Positive Affirmations

Many people look down on positive affirmations but the truth is that they are very effective when used in the right way. A little earlier we talked about the fact that the brain learns via repetition. That is exactly what a positive affirmation does - you repeat a statement regularly until your brain takes it on board as fact.

The difference here is that you have to believe in the statement you are repeating. It is no good trying to tell yourself that you are a duck or a cow and repeating it, expecting to believe it - your brain is very sophisticated and it can tell the difference between total nonsense and things that could be true! For that reason, you need to spend some time thinking about an

166

affirmation that you believe in or want to believe in, and that resonates with what you're trying to achieve.

Once you have chosen your affirmation, you need to spend some time every day repeating it. Visualize the words as you say them and they will resonate more clearly. When you wake up in the morning, repeat your affirmation three times. It is best to say the words aloud if you can and close your eyes so you can see the words as you say them. Then, do the same thing again mid-morning and again before bed. If you feel you need to repeat the words once more throughout the day, do so. You could also put the words somewhere visible throughout the day, such as your cell phone background or stick them to your laptop screen.

Studies have shown[9] that positive affirmations work very well when you dedicate yourself to using them correctly. Again, it is not going to change your mindset overnight but it could bring very positive changes to your life if given a little extra time to work. There is no actual timeline here, as every single person is different and will have a specific amount of negativity to push out of their life. It's also useful to try other strategies alongside affirmations, such as mindfulness or reframing, which we're about to talk about a little more.

Mindfulness

Mindfulness has become somewhat of a buzzword over the last few years, for a very good reason. The ability to live in the present day, without dwelling in the past or worrying about the future can have major benefits. Mindfulness has been shown to improve mental health[10] and with that, comes the chance to improve positivity and all of this links into developing that lucky mentality.

Of course, becoming more mindful is another element that doesn't happen overnight. We are all so concerned with what has been and gone and what is to come that we don't tend to enjoy the present day. When you are trying to encourage new opportunities into your life, mindfulness is key because you need to be on the lookout for those signs, otherwise you will miss them. If you are not mindful, it means opportunities are passing you by right now. When you master the art of mindfulness, you can simply observe life and accept it for what it is. That doesn't mean you never take action, it means that you wait for the right moment and you allow your emotions to settle rather than acting out of anger, sadness, desperation, or other heightened and negative emotions.

Your breath is the one thing you can rely upon throughout life. You are born with it and you die when it ends. That means it is always there for you. When you need to calm down or clear your mind, close your eyes and focus on your breathing. Learning to meditate can be a great help for this. Although meditation also takes a lot of practice, you have one very effective tool at your disposal; breathing.

You should never expect your mind to fall silent and to be able to be completely clear of all noise and thoughts. That is a fallacy about meditation. People feel like they are failing because they are not able to completely silence their minds but that is not possible, or at least not until you are a meditation expert! Instead, you need to feel comfortable allowing thoughts to drift in and out, without the need to react or act upon them immediately. When you are trying to be mindful and you notice your thoughts pulling you in another direction, focus on your breathing and it will help to ground you. All of this is extremely useful when trying to develop a more positive mindset. Not feeling stressed out about the past or future, and not being at the mercy of your emotions is a wonderfully freeing experience.

As you are walking around during the day or going about your daily tasks, try and focus on the small details. For instance, when you are out walking the dog, focus on the way the leaves blow in the breeze, the clouds moving in the sky, the way your dog bounds up happily to greet you when you throw a ball for them. Pay attention to the small details that you would normally miss and you will be far more grounded in the present.

By practising this over time, you will learn to accept things as they are, rather than trying to desperately change and manipulate everything. All of this helps you to be more relaxed, more positive, and generally happier.

Reframing

Reframing is a cognitive behavioural therapy technique (CBT) that is used to help change negatives into positives throughout a range of different mental health and behavioural conditions. However, you can also make very good use of this technique by simply becoming a more positive person. When you reframe, you basically take a negative thought, accept it as being negative, and then turn it into something positive. You then use the art of repetition to teach your brain to recognize the positive before the negative. Again, this requires you to be mindful of your thoughts. You need to pick up on a thought and say to yourself "that was negative", which then triggers you to transfer it to the positive side of the spectrum.

The key is to look for the lesson. For instance, presentations are probably never going to be anyone's favourite task, but they do allow you to practice public speaking and therefore become more confident. They also allow you to shine, which could help your boss to pinpoint you for promotion next time around. Dragging your self-confidence down by talking negatively about your body doesn't help you, but identifying your body as the strong and healthy thing that it is, will help you to see the truth of the matter. By doing that, you build your confidence and you are more able to see new opportunities that arise. This could push you to go out and meet new people, refusing to let body confidence issues drag you down.

The same can be said for something as simple as saying that you hate the rain. That may mean that whenever it rains, you just don't go outside. How do you know that you are not missing out on a wonderful opportunity because you decided to let a little rain keep you indoors? I adore the rain; I feel my heart dance from inside when it rains! So, not only does reframing help you to become more positive as a default, but it also helps to boost your confidence to get out to grab more opportunities. This in itself helps you to develop that all-important lucky mentality we have been talking about.

Once you have identified the positive thought you want to reframe the negative one with, you need to repeat it. Just the same as with positive affirmations, it is best to repeat it aloud and to close your eyes and visualize if you can. This adds extra weight to what you are trying to achieve. Picture the new, positive thought in your mind and continue to repeat the new thought whenever it pops into your head again. Over time your brain will recognize the new, reframed thought before the old, negative one. It takes time, and it won't happen immediately, but once you start to see progress, you will be encouraged to carry on.

The truth is as simple as this - when you are a positive person, you see the world differently. You look for opportunities and when one pops up, you are more likely to take it. You are potentially creating your own luck because without that 'go get it' attitude, you are just going to be stuck where you are, not encouraging any fresh energy into your life. The other advantage is that positive thinking makes you happier and healthier. You can start on your new positive thinking adventure right now. Simply remember that you are not going to wake up tomorrow morning and suddenly start seeing the glass as half full - it may take a while, but you will get there in the end and you will be thankful that you put in the effort.

Habits of lucky people

The lucky mentality school emphasis building that lucky mentality which helps to bring a wealth of new opportunities into your life. From there, you can take advantage of the ones that you feel suit you best and as a result, you are making your own luck. That doesn't rule out chance occurrences of course, but those are the things you have no control over. Being in the right place at the right time does require you to get out and about in the first place, so even taking into account the chance encounters, you are on the right track to be where you need to be.

In addition to having the right mentality, 'lucky' people also have specific habits[11] that they use daily, mostly without even realizing. It is not possible to develop positive habits that encourage luck without having that positive and lucky mentality. They work hand in hand, so first, you need to focus on developing the mentality and then you need to cultivate some positive daily habits. In this section, we are going to explore the habits of lucky people and explain how you can develop the habit as your own. It may be that you already have some of the habits we are going to talk about, but perhaps you need to focus on them a little more or utilize positive thinking alongside them. Be mindful of the habits you already have and be open to adding more. Also, don't take it personally if you do need to work on specific areas. Nobody is perfect and there is always room for improvement!

You can choose to work on several at once or you can dedicate your time to one and then move on to another when you feel like you have started to make headway. What you shouldn't do is overload yourself and try and work on them all at one time. Take things slowly and know that any progress is better than none.

Habit 1 - "Lucky" people have an optimistic outlook on life

We spent a lot of time in our last section talking about positivity, but optimism is a slightly different thing. Yes, the two are connected and you do need to be positive to be optimistic, but if you want to develop a lucky mentality, you need to learn to look for the best in life and expect it to come your way. Lucky people believe that they are lucky. In so many ways it is a trick of the mind because when you believe something is going to happen, you tend to notice that it is far more likely. Again, it comes down to making things happen yourself, looking for opportunities and being more open to taking them.

Being positive means believing that everything is going to work out for you. On the other hand, optimism means that you accept things as they are. You don't worry about the things that aren't so perfect and instead, you accept the negative along with the positive. You know that everything will work out and that you don't have to fear anything.

Part of the lucky mentality is being able to accept life as it is and looking for the best in any situation. Of course, that is not always easy. For instance, if you lose your job, the first thing you are going to do is panic about how you are going to pay the bills. This is normal. Once the waters settle, an optimistic person will look for the lesson and focus on a better future. They might see losing their job as an opportunity to get a better job or to perhaps change their career completely. They know that they may face obstacles along the way and they don't expect everything to be perfect but they have faith that it will work out.

So, how can you learn to be more optimistic? There are a few things you can try. You can look at your inner circle - Who you spend the majority of your time with can have a huge impact on your mentality. We tend to mimic those around us without even realizing it, so if you're spending a lot of time around someone who is quite negative and has a 'we're all doomed' outlook on life, you are going to find it hard to think positive. It may be that you can't completely kick these people out of your life, and you probably don't even want to, but you can minimize the amount of time you spend with naysayers and spend more time with other optimists. You will probably find that optimism catches on. You can also try to be a more positive person - I won't dwell on this too much as we spent a lot of time exploring how to become a more positive person in our last section. However, working towards positivity can help you become more optimistic. The two indeed work hand in hand and without one, you can't have the other one.

You need also to understand that negatives happen to balance out the positives. There will always be negatives in life. You can't expect everything to be roses and rainbows. However, the negatives are there to help us learn and improve and to do better next time. An optimistic person won't try to shy away from the negatives. They don't particularly enjoy them but they accept them as they are and they don't panic about trying to change them. This is part and parcel of mindfulness, something we have already explored a little earlier on. By learning to be more mindful, you can accept the things in life that happen without the need to do anything about them. Sometimes we can't put a positive spin on something, it is just impossible, but we can accept it and know that it all adds to the balance of life.

You need also to cut down on the amount of news you watch - he is important. It is not easy to be optimistic when you are surrounded by negative news, doom and gloom. Just as I mentioned not spending a huge amount of time with those who are always negative, you have to try and limit the amount of negative news you watch too. This can affect your mood and mindset very dramatically. Know that any important news you need to know about will come to your attention, and you don't need to constantly check news apps and programs to learn what is going on in the world.

You can be more optimistic by not trying to plan so much for the future. It is normal to have goals and ideas for the future but when you start planning everything out to the letter, it is not going to help you become more optimistic or happier. Being too focused on the future can cause anxiety. You forget to enjoy the here and now and you create problems thinking about the 'what-ifs'. The best thing here is mindfulness once more. Sure, have goals, it is important to have something to work towards and it is a great way to be optimistic in itself, but you don't have to be so in control that a rigid plan is always in place. You can't enjoy the ride of life and welcome luck into your days if you are focused on what you're going to do every single minute, without any lee-way!

One way to be more optimistic is to understand your limitations. Having an 'I can do anything I put my mind to' mindset is a good thing in some ways but it doesn't teach you that you have limits. Everyone has limits, even the most intelligent, successful people on the planet. There are some things that you just can't control or change. Part of becoming more optimistic is learning to accept the things that you can't do anything about and just going with it, having faith that things will work out. It is not easy to do, but having a positive mindset will make it easier. Affirmations could help you with this task too, so choose something that has a calming element, such as "I am calm and going with the flow", or "I am strong enough to deal with anything life throws at me".

Will becoming more optimistic alone make you luckier? Probably not. However, it will help you to be happier and calmer in your life and thus more able to take advantage of opportunities that come your way.

Habit 2 - "Lucky" people are do-ers

One common habit of a lucky person is proactivity. This is someone who does things. They don't sit around and wait for things to happen or weigh up the pros and cons and decide to just wait a little more and see how the land lies later. They make a decision and they see it through. That doesn't mean they are reckless and gung-ho in their decision making but they don't dither over their decisions either.

This is probably one of the most important habits to try and develop if you want to have that all-important lucky mentality.

It is not just about being able to see opportunities that come your way, it is also about being brave enough to take them. This may be difficult if you are a reserved and shy person, or if you have suffered a setback in the past after seizing an opportunity. Being proactive means seeing an opportunity and deciding whether to take it or not. If it is not the opportunity for you, don't take it. You don't have to jump on board with everything that comes your way. However, if you listen to your intuition and it is telling you that perhaps this could be a good thing for you, go for it.

Taking small, measured risks can help you to become more proactive over time. Start small, and when that works out for you, take a larger chance. Follow this pattern and soon you will be someone who doesn't overthink things before taking an opportunity. If part and parcel of being lucky is simply being in the right place at the right time, then being proactive will help you get up and grab those opportunities. If you sit around and wait for too long, someone else will take that chance away from you!

Habit 3 - "Lucky" people are mindful

That word again - mindfulness! Whilst so-called lucky people may not outwardly practice mindfulness in terms of meditation and other exercises, they are generally quite mindful in their natural day to day life. They don't tend to worry too much about what has been and gone, and they don't worry too much about the future. Instead, they are open to changes that come their way and whilst they might have a goal or two, they are working towards, they are willing to deviate from their original plans to accommodate something better. Living in the moment sounds easy but in practice, it's quite difficult if you are someone who is always thinking backwards or forwards. Having something to work on is a good way to keep your mind focused but again, meditation is a very positive thing to try too. A little earlier we talked about being mindful of your surroundings when out and about walking - that is a mindful meditation exercise that you can do without ever having tried the "regular" type of meditation in the past.

You can also try and recognize when you are starting to think back over past events or jump forward and worry about the future. When you notice that you are doing it, pull yourself back to the future and focus on what is in front of you. Some people like to shock themselves back to the present, perhaps with an elastic band on their wrist. However, it may be enough to simply say "no" very firmly to yourself and refocus your mind that way. See what works for you, we are all different and certain practices may work better for you than it does for others. However, becoming more mindful will help you in so many different elements of your life. Then, when an opportunity comes your way, you will be able to examine it without worrying and jumping into the old habit of proactivity!

Habit 4 - "Lucky" people are insightful

Being able to read a person or a specific situation as it arises can sometimes be difficult if you find it hard to focus your mind. A negative person will probably always jump to a negative conclusion, perhaps overlooking the good and positive possibilities of the situation. Lucky people combine positivity and insightfulness, they can read situations and are quite perceptive, without allowing their judgment or past experiences to interfere. This is probably one of the hardest habits to develop but that doesn't mean it is impossible! By being more insightful, you will certainly boost the relationships you have with those around you and you will find that you make better decisions too.

So, how can you learn to be more insightful? This one may take some time, but here are some tactics you can try. First, you need to read more. An insightful person has knowledge. That doesn't mean they have a high IQ; it means they enjoy learning and absorbing new information. I mentioned not watching the news too often a little earlier (if you want to become a more optimistic person), but you can look for subjects you are interested in and read more about those. You have the internet at your fingertips so you have no excuse! You could also try having conversations with people about subjects you are interested in and listen to their point of view. We can all learn from one another.

Secondly, you need to learn to listen. Far too many people assume that listening is just a case of allowing words to enter the ears. That is not even part of the process. Real listening, or active listening as it is often called, involves not just hearing the words but deciphering what they mean. Learn to listen to people's words, how they are speaking, and the tone they are using, the volume, and pitch, and then look at their body language too. All of this will help you to become a better listener because you can read between the lines and understand the person much better. You should also avoid interrupting when someone is speaking.

Thirdly, you need to work on your empathy skills. Becoming more empathetic is so beneficial on many levels but in terms of being insightful, it is probably one of the best things to work on. When you have empathy, you can see things from another person's perspective and you can literally "walk a mile in their shoes". Being able to listen properly will help you to develop your empathy. A good starting point is to try to explore how a person may be feeling by asking yourself how you would feel in their situation. Listen, read their body language, don't make assumptions, and try to understand the bigger picture. All of this will help you to become a more empathetic and insightful person.

Fourthly, don't make it all about you – It is not possible to be an insightful person if you make everything about yourself. Perhaps you do this without realizing it, but try to consider others' feelings a little more. When you are insular and only think of yourself, perhaps because you are worried about something or you are going through a hard time, you become blind to everything going on around you. In such a situation, how are you supposed to see potential opportunities that could bring good fortune your way?

Habit 5 - "Lucky" people know an opportunity when they see it

You could call this being opportunistic but a so-called lucky person can recognize an opportunity. To you, it may just be a chance offering or event, but to someone with an opportunistic mindset, small offerings can turn into major chances. This doesn't mean that every small thing that comes your way is a golden ticket, but it does mean being able to see the bigger picture. What are the chances that this could turn into something larger? What could help it get to somewhere better than where it is right now? Of course, some things you can't read or predict, but having an open mind will allow you to see good opportunities.

You can start small with this and build up. So, if someone asks you to go to a dinner party with them, rather than just turning it down because you don't know anyone, be open to the chance that you could meet some new people and have a great time. You may not enjoy it, but at least you took a step out of your comfort zone and tried something new. However, there is the possibility that you might meet a new friend, perhaps a new romantic interest, or possibly someone who has connections in the type of career you are trying to get into.

An opportunistic person can recognize how a small opportunity can turn into something much larger and will be brave enough to attempt it.

Habit 6 - "Lucky" people don't give up easily

Resilience and flexibility are two very strong traits in 'lucky' people. If you are too rigid, you will miss out on opportunities lying off the track you have tied yourself to. If you give up too easily, you are never going to know what may have happened if you would just stick with it a little longer.

Negativity is the main cause of rigidity and giving up quickly. Try to be a little more accommodating and don't just stick to the same schedule every day. If someone says "hey, let us go to a different restaurant this evening", or "let's drive to the next city and try that Arabic restaurant everyone is talking about", consider what new personal and professional opportunities could come your way through this experience. Can you see how being flexible and opportunistic ties in with one another?

Being flexible also means that you are accommodating the needs of others, which could help with your empathy skills too. All of these habits link to one another but you need to be able to work on each one separately, to get the complete picture. Whenever something you are working on hits a bump, don't automatically assume that it is not going to work out and just give up. Instead, look for the lessons. What are you doing wrong or what could be changed or done better? How can you take the current situation and improve it? Often, it only takes small tweaks to smooth over that bump! You could even ask the advice of someone close to you. Ask them what they would do in your situation; how would they approach the problem? You don't have to take their advice but you can consider it and perhaps pick parts from it to form your next move. The point is that you are not just throwing in the towel and moving on to the next thing, you are being resilient and refusing to give in.

If being flexible and resilient are two of the main habits of a so-called lucky person, the good news is that you can develop those habits for yourself with practice. All you need to do is catch yourself being rigid or lacking resilience in the future and force yourself to try a new route. Quickly enough you will see that taking a chance doesn't lead to disaster and if anything, it could lead to something wonderful.

Habit 7 - "Lucky" people see things from all angles

You have no doubt heard the saying "think outside of the box", but what does that mean? Generally speaking, it means being able to see things from many different angles. Dare to allow your creativity to take your mind places it has never been before. When you do that, you will make more creative and innovative decisions, but you may also be able to carve out opportunities for yourself without evening realizing it. The next time you need to make a decision don't jump straight into it. Rather wait for a little. Give yourself some time to explore your options, because they are probably far more wide-reaching than you could know at the time. You could even write down a list if that helps you, and be as creative as possible. You can always scratch a few off the list if they seem a little too far-fetched!

Once you have a list of options, don't automatically go with the safest one. Just because it seems safer doesn't mean it is the right choice. This is where your intuition will certainly help you out but you can ask for opinions from other people too. Again, sometimes asking for different viewpoints can help you to unlock ideas in your mind that would otherwise have stayed under lock and key. It is easy to stay in your comfort zone and go for the easiest option or avoid deciding at all but that is not going to bring new opportunities into your life. If you want to open your life up to new adventures then you are going to have to help things along and do things that have been alien to you up until now. It may seem scary at first, but it is the same as everything else in life - the more you do it, the easier it becomes.

These habits are all things that so-called lucky people tend to have and do regularly. Most of these they employ daily without even realizing it. These habits have become second nature and part of their character. However, just because you haven't had these traits or habits in your life regularly so far doesn't mean you can't welcome them into your space now. You will need to be very aware of your thoughts and actions for a while and you will have to do things that feel very awkward or different to you. The reward is a healthier, happier life with increased chances of new opportunities and adventures coming your way.

Chapter 7
Luck Of The Irish

Luck Of The Irish

I have been always fascinated with Ireland and its natural beauty. As a child growing up in the ancient Syrian city of Aleppo, I used to look at the atlas of the world given to me by my father, who was a teacher and I used to go through and examine each city on this beautiful island. I used to search the local school library for pictures of Ireland, back then in the late1980s, we did not have uncle Google to help us as the internet did not exist. It was such a hard task yet I managed to collect a couple of breath-taking pictures of Ireland.

During my student years in Manchester, I met some Irish friends for the first time in my life, and they proved to me that the natural beauty of Ireland and the kindness of its people go hand in hand.

In 2018, I had the honour of finally visiting Ireland, to search for my luck. I went there trying to buy Irish prize bonds, which rewards its holder with a chance to win €250,000 four times a year and up to €50,000 in weekly draws. I collected all the required papers, filled in the application but then I could not proceed because opening an Irish bank account was nearly impossible if you were not a resident. Nevertheless, this visit left me even more charmed by this captivating land and its eternally cheerful people.

Of all the people in the world, it is perhaps the Irish who are most commonly associated with luck. Their rich culture and heritage have many ties to luck, from leprechauns and lucky clovers to the old expression 'luck of the Irish'. Yet, where does the term come from? With so many references to luck in Irish culture, it can be difficult to figure out where the term originated. Fortunately, the term is surprisingly recent it seems, and its origin is not only easier to trace than you might expect, but also much different to what most would assume.

The most likely origin of the phrase 'luck of the Irish' originated with Irish good fortune in the mines of 19th century America, but this does not necessarily mean it is correct. There are many other potential reasons why people have come to consider the Irish to be blessed with good luck, ranging from their rich heritage of folktales to simply being more likeable due to their accent. A study from The Knowledge Academy found that 77% of the women studied found the Irish accent to be one of the most appealing accents in the world[1,] which may also account for the Irish being considered lucky by others. Nonetheless, it is worth looking at some of the other historical or cultural reasons why the Irish are considered lucky.

The old mining terms

The term 'luck of the Irish' was coined during the early 19th century in America, and despite it having positive connotations today, it was originally used in a derogatory manner[2]. During the great potato famine in Ireland, many Irish immigrants moved to America in search of a better life, and many of them found work in the mining industry. Perhaps driven by the journey they had taken and the desire for a new life in America, the Irish immigrants were generally harder workers than their American counterparts. Given that they also arrived during America's gold rush period, it didn't take long for the immigrants to start seeing success in their mining endeavours.

So, why was their success put down to luck as opposed to hard work and perseverance? It was an attempt by local Americans to degrade the talent of the immigrants. In a time where everyone was competing for their fortune, it would have negatively impacted locals to have their skills called into question compared to Irish immigrants. While being naturally 'lucky' still put the immigrant miners ahead of them, it helped locals to save face when compared with their competitors. Blaming luck for their comparative lack of success, rather than their own lack of perseverance, made it easier for them to accept the success of the Irish miners. Not surprisingly, using 'luck' to excuse personal failures is a common behaviour[3], and has been for centuries.

While at first luck was only attributed to some individuals, many of whom just happened to be from Ireland, the fact is that many of the most successful and even most famous miners were either of Irish or American-Irish descent. This is why the term 'the luck of the Irish' became popular and while good luck is considered to be a good thing by many people today, it was originally used with derision. It conveyed the message that the Irish miners only succeeded by sheer luck because they had neither the brains nor brawn to compete with American miners on equal ground[4].

Fortunately, the phrase's meaning changed drastically over the years and is now considered to have positive connotations. After having seen so many Irish miners succeed over the years, and hearing the phrase for so long, it is understandable that people began to genuinely believe that the Irish were blessed with good luck.

The 'bad' luck of the Irish

Throughout history, the Irish people suffered many catastrophes and disasters, and the term 'luck of the Irish' itself makes no differentiation between 'good' or 'bad' luck.

Even at the height of the gold rush era, during which many Irish immigrants found their fortune, countless had to fight prejudice and racism. The good luck of a few led to locals looking poorly on their people as a whole, which certainly would not be considered good luck for the vast majority of the Irish. The reason for their arrival in America to begin with, the great potato famine, was perhaps one of the best-known disasters in Irish history and certainly does nothing to support the Irish people's purported penchant for good luck. The Great Famine was a time of tragedy for the whole country, impacting both the health and wealth of the country to such a degree that it is a wonder they ever recovered at all[5].

Even before the Great Famine, there were significant struggles and upheaval in Ireland, along with a multitude of other problems. Considering that the country is an island it should be easily defensible, it should have been fortunate enough to fend off invaders successfully time and time again. As a comparative example, Japan, a fellow island nation, was never successfully invaded until the American occupation during World War II. Yet centuries before this war, Ireland had already struggled with invasion and found itself unable to defend itself. Ireland was already struggling with invaders in the first millennium, as Vikings made their way into the country. The first recorded incident appears to have taken place in roughly 795 AD[6], at which point the Vikings successfully looted Lambay, which lead to even more looting.

Ginger hair and luck!

The Irish seems to be more commonly born with red/ginger hair thanks to the high prevalence of the V60L allele, also informally known as the 'ginger gene', in their genome. According to a study by Dr Saioa Lopez, approximately 10% of the Irish population are born with this gene, compared with roughly 2% of people from other nations. This often leads to paler skin, and as a result, the Irish are more susceptible to melanoma and other similar conditions[7] which once again exposes the Irish to potential bad luck.

These health risks are not the only downside to red hair. Those who were born with ginger hair were marked as 'different' throughout history, and frequently in a negative light. One example would be the reference to red-haired people in the Malleus Malefic arum (often translated as Hammer of Witches), the best-known treatise on witchcraft. This treatise identified redheads as people of particular interest in the search for witches and other non-human entities hiding amongst humans! In particular, redheads were generally considered to be vampires, no doubt in part due to their pale skin making them more vulnerable to sunlight - much like vampires. The treatise read "Those whose hair is red, of a certain peculiar shade, are unmistakably vampires". This would have left those with red hair, frequently Irish, at a higher risk of being hunted on suspicion of vampirism.

This discrimination was not even necessarily the most notable of incidents where redheads were targeted, as even without being a direct target, they could find themselves labelled as potential threats, due to their high incidence of red hair.

During the Spanish Inquisition, which started after the fall of Granada in 1492 AD and resulting in the ending of nearly 800 years of Muslim rule in Spain, many Irish people were incorrectly identified as Jewish and marked for isolation and persecution[8]. This idea that red-haired people were Jewish came primarily from the common representation of Judas, who would often be depicted in artwork with red hair. These are only a few examples of the troubles the Irish faced over the centuries, all of which together do very little to support the idea that the Irish are 'lucky'. In fact, they seem decidedly unlucky, and it could be considered that this is another potential origin for the term 'the luck of the Irish'.

It is entirely plausible that the term does not refer to good luck but instead relates to the many misfortunes that have befallen the Irish people over the centuries. Although it is common to read the phrase as referring to good luck, it may be wiser to consider it a misnomer, while this is not generally the accepted origin for the term 'the luck of the Irish' it is still worth considering this alternative meaning as the possible original meaning for the term.

The four-leaf clover

One of the more peculiar Irish symbols is the four-leaf clover, as it is arguably something of an Irish icon and is a common symbol in both Irish mythology and folklore. But what exactly is it? The four-leaf clover is a plant that grows abundantly on the island of Ireland and around the areas where Irish people call home. However, this does not mean that it cannot grow elsewhere in the world, as they are found all over the globe. The origins of the luck association of four-leaf clover are still a mystery. However, most people believe that the plant was brought to the USA and particularly California by immigrants from Europe. It is not known where or when exactly this happened, but there are many examples found in California dating back to the year 1900! Some have speculated that 'the four-leaf clover' is not simply a reference to 'good luck' for the Irish but instead refers to the plant being lucky in general. However, this is far from the universal consensus and so it may be wise to consider an alternative meaning for this symbol. The four-leaf clover is thought to be lucky for different reasons, the first is its rarity, and the second is its usage by Druid priests to treat and heal the sick and to ward off the evil spirits. In ancient Egypt, married couples were given a four-leaf clover as a sign of blessing for their marriage.

Some legends even date the story of the four-leaf clover to Adam and Eve, where Eve carried it with her from the Garden of Eden to be reminded of the bliss of Paradise, and so if you have one, you will be having a piece from paradise itself.

We should consider that the two meanings of 'luck' can be applied to people and things alike. This would mean that it is not just the Irish who are lucky in terms of their people being fortunate, but also that other things such as the four-leaf clover can be considered 'lucky'. This fits well with how the phrase 'the luck of the Irish' is often used to refer to a person being lucky. One popular theory that could be explored here would be that the four-leaf clover was once considered lucky because it only rarely emerges on its own. It appears that a four-leaf clover typically requires fertiliser to grow, which would make it all the more impressive if a four-leaf clover were to grow naturally. By taking this approach, the four-leaf clover could then be considered a 'lucky' symbol just like the Irish are, as they are both rare occurrences. This is not a definitive answer to finding the true meaning of 'the luck of the Irish', but it may help shed some light on what it could have originally meant.

The four-leaf clover is known by many names. Some of these include the shamrock, harnack, ceann dubh, black spade and the gaol Mai. However, these may vary depending on the region of the country you are speaking about and what language you are using. While the majority of people refer to it as a 'four-leaf clover', this term is not specific to Ireland. It can also be found in many countries, such as England and Scotland.

The four-leaf clover has become an emblem for Ireland and as such, it has become something of an Irish icon that many people recognise instantly. There is even an Irish story about the four-leaf clover. Since it has become an Irish icon and well recognised-image, many people have attempted to

194

commercialise the four-leaf clover in various ways. This includes growing the plant abundantly and selling it to companies wishing to bolster their Irish heritage. There are actually a couple of businesses that have grown the four-leaf clover commercially in Ireland.

The four-leaf clover has become quite a popular symbol for various Irish souvenirs as well as many Irish commercial ventures. Some people even use it to spell out their names and, in some cases, it is even used to represent Ireland itself. This is a symbol that has been around for hundreds of years. However, it remains just as prominent today as it ever was. The four-leaf clover is a part of Irish folklore and culture, and it will continue to be so.

On the other hand, some Irish believe that finding a clover with 5 or more leaves is unlucky!

Leprechauns

Although some Irish people may claim that their ancestors had some magical abilities bestowed upon them by the leprechauns, there is little evidence to back this up. As with many of the phrases above, the fact that leprechauns are a common element of Irish legend does not indicate that this at least makes it a likely origin of the 'luck of the Irish' phrase. There are several other possible origins for the phrase.

What is a Leprechaun?

Leprechauns are probably best known for their role in Irish legends and folklore, appearing in stories as the guardians of pots of gold, often with some sort of magical ability. Although the idea of 'luck bestowed by a leprechaun' has a certain appeal when considering the origin of 'the luck of the Irish', it should not be automatically assumed that any mention or depiction of leprechauns in popular culture indicates that it is based on the Irish people's association with good luck. Although leprechauns are often considered to be evil, there is no evidence to suggest that they were inherently evil. The most common depiction of a leprechaun is that of the small, red-headed, cackling man with a keen interest in gold often seen in Irish folklore and storytelling. As a result, it has been suggested that the Irish were attracted to this character, to have a totem by which they could remember or symbolise their connection with luck.

It is important to note that although leprechauns are part of Irish folklore, they were not introduced by Ireland itself. The supposed invention of leprechauns can be traced back to Ireland's sister nation, Holland, where in the 1650's, a book was written by Johannes Brandt which depicted leprechauns as little men of around one foot tall who shared their love of gold and beer with the Dutch people.

Many other European countries have also claimed to have invented leprechauns, most notably Scotland which seems to provide a large part of the inspiration for these little creatures. There seems to be no reason why Ireland could not have created its own version of this being, although there is little evidence to suggest that they did. Thus, the origin of leprechauns may be rooted in many different places, however, just as it is possible that leprechauns originated in Ireland, it is also possible that their appearance could have coined the phrase "the luck of the Irish". Whether or not they had any influence over this phrase, leprechauns are still an intrinsic part of Irish culture and as such are more than capable of influencing the nation's folklore.

The leprechaun in popular culture

Leprechauns have recently become a relatively common feature in popular culture, particularly in America where they have been used as mascots for events such as the Kentucky Derby, various sports games and even for police officers. In all of these cases, it would be unusual to claim that these associations were intended to encourage luck amongst the Irish populace but instead are simply attempts to use the popularity of leprechauns to attract attention. In fact, it is very unlikely that the people involved in these operations would even consider 'the luck of the Irish' as an explanation for their use of the leprechaun symbol.

Despite all the above attempts to explain the origin of the famous 'luck of the Irish ', they are not definitive answers for how this phrase came about. For this reason, I believe it may still be best to treat 'the luck of the Irish' as a cryptic phrase that is never to be taken at face value.

St. Patrick's Day

Another major day in the Irish calendar is St Patrick's Day, which takes place on March 17th. This day commemorates the death of Ireland's patron saint, St Patrick and is therefore marked as a very important day in the history of Ireland itself.

It is likely that St Patrick's Day was not widely celebrated outside of Ireland until the Protestant Reformation, when those wishing to distance themselves from the Roman Catholic Church adopted this as a day to celebrate their faith. St Patrick's day also marked the beginning of Lent in Ireland, which for some Christians is a religiously crucial time.

According to legend, St. Patrick himself used a three-leaf clover as part of his teachings, as it helped explain the concept of the Holy Trinity.

Irish Harp

Bizarrely, it has also been suggested that the Irish harp is a symbol of Irish luck and success.

This idea arises from the fact that far more ancient versions of the instrument appear on gravestones in Scotland, Ireland and Wales. It has been suggested that these engravings represent a belief in reincarnation – where the deceased hope for their next life to be a successful one. It is certainly an interesting theory that relies heavily on the interpretation of ancient gravestones rather than modern evidence or facts.

Another significant aspect of the harp in Ireland is its role in storytelling. The story of the harp is a long one, and includes many historical details, but remains relevant to this day - especially when considering the 'luck of the Irish'. In brief, the harp was a gift from an unnamed nobleman to King Cormac

Mac Art (circa 2nd century). This nobleman died during a great famine, and so his wife sent his servant to deliver his harp as a gift to Cormac's daughter. However, this servant fell in love with Cormac's daughter and instead accepted her ring as payment for the harp. Unfortunately, the servant was caught and murdered by Cormac's men. He did not die since the harp played for him all through the night - granting him a reprieve from death, and also bringing hope to his wife who also spent all night playing music to keep her husband alive. Based on this legend, it is quite common for people in Ireland to consider playing the harp (or even just listening to it) a sign of good luck.

Shamrock

Another prominent symbol associated with the Irish people would be the shamrock. This is the most well-known of all Irish symbols, and it is commonly accepted that it represents Saint Patrick teaching people about the Holy Trinity. Christians believe that there are three components to the living God, those being the Father, the Son and the Holy Spirit. The symbol of the shamrock represents these three components as it is a tri-leafed clover. The shamrock is often seen on St. Patrick's Day and has since become a national symbol for Irish people worldwide.

'Luck of the Irish' in films

In 1948, a film was directed by Henry Koster and produced by Fred Kohlmar named the luck of the Irish. The plot is about Stephen Fitzgerald, a newspaper reporter from New York, who meets a leprechaun and the beautiful young Nora, while in Ireland. When he returns to his fiancée Frances and her wealthy father, he finds that the leprechaun and Nora are now in the big city as well. Stephen is torn between the wealth he might enjoy in New York or returning to his roots in Ireland.

In 2001, the Disney Channel produced a film also named The Luck of the Irish. It is about 15-year-old basketball player Kyle Johnson who relies on a gold charm for luck. He learns that he has leprechaun ancestry on his mother's side and must find out how to get their leprechaun power back to break a spell controlled by an evil leprechaun named Seamus McTiernan.

The luck of the Irish today

Although it is unclear exactly when the phrase started to come into common use, it is used frequently enough to appear in the Merriam-Webster dictionary. Today, the use of the term comes with a variety of different examples. Many people are aware of the Irish-American contribution to American politics, and this is perhaps one example of the 'luck' that they are said to have brought to the USA. Mother Jones, Eugene O'Neill and the famous Kennedy family in the US were all of Irish descent and they contributed massively to the progress and well-being of the United States by bringing their Irish luck to the new land. The band U2's Bono (Paul David Hewson) who is a famous Irish singer, songwriter and businessman has been labelled by Time magazine as one of the most influential people of 2005. Amongst many other achievements, the band were also awarded The Golden Globe Award for best original song score for their work on the soundtrack for the movie Gangs of New York.

William John Neeson, more commonly known as Liam Neeson, is a famous Irish actor and is my all-time favourite actor. He has contributed considerably to the world of films worldwide. The Irish are also famous for their achievements in football. The Dublin born and Ireland international team player, Robbie Keane, is but one example.

Irish music as a vehicle of good luck

One of the most notable cultural traditions in Irish culture, and one which makes Ireland more than just a simple geographic location, is its music. Music is a recurring theme throughout Irish culture and has had a significant impact on the country as a whole. There are many different forms of music native to Ireland, including traditional music and folk music. The traditional forms of Irish music include Céilidh (a type of Irish folk dance), fiddle tunes (Irish musical notation) and tunes from the Irish folk song tradition. Many cultural traditions in Ireland involve music and Ireland is often called the 'home of music'. The musical traditions of Ireland also extend far beyond traditional music and folk songs and even include modern pop music. One of the most notable examples of this is the group U2, who hail from Ireland and are well-known for their songs 'With or Without you' and 'I Still Haven't Found What I'm Looking for'. Although their music is not purely Irish in origin, they have had an immensely positive impact on Irish culture.

The Irish have also had a significant influence on modern popular music with some of the most successful artists being based in Dublin. Irish music has also had a notable influence on other genres, for example, the popular jazz musician Miles

Davis began experimenting with Irish folk music when he lived in Dublin. He drew heavily on the influence of this music for his later work. Dolores O'Riordan comes to mind as the lead vocalist and lyricist for the alternative rock band the Cranberries. Thin Lizzy and the Dubliners, the famous Irish folk band are also great popular Irish bands. Let us not forget also the Corrs .

In addition to this, folk and modern pop artists such as Enya and Bono have had a significant impact on international popularity within their respective genres. The large variety of music in Ireland has kept it culturally diverse and has also promoted a cultural appreciation for diversity. This diversity has helped Ireland to develop a unique culture, which is characterized by music, dance and the celebration of St. Patrick's Day.

Even the famous Irish dance carries with it a sense of happiness, good fortune, and vibes of bliss. There are many reasons why Irish culture with its Gaelic heritage and captivating music has become so popular throughout the world. First of all, Ireland has been recognized as one of the most beautiful countries in Europe, so tourists come from around the world to visit places such as Dublin or Galway. It is also the land where Celtic culture is at its strongest and Ireland has a large population of Goidelic speakers (especially in the North). Another reason why Irish culture is so popular is that it has become accessible to people who may be resistant to other elements of European culture. Traditional Irish culture has not been tainted by religious and political conflicts in recent memory and the immersion of Irish music into modern music has helped make it more popular and accessible than ever before.

The Irish and Luck in Popular Culture

The Irish have also had a significant impact on world culture in their influence on the English language. In America for example, the word 'lucky' has become part of popular vocabulary, with the American definition being very similar to that of the Irish. For example, someone might say they are looking for a good job and not finding any luck. This use of 'luck' often refers to making an effort and then receiving favourable results as a reward, proving that it has been adopted into day-to-day language with its original meaning. This also shows us that despite the negative undertone inherent in many uses of this phrase, it has been incorporated into our everyday vocabulary as a positive term.

The luck of the Irish in America

The aforementioned treatment of the Irish in America is a prime example of the supposed luck of the Irish, as they have managed to find success and fortune across the Atlantic. This was not always guaranteed, as there was a period after the Great Potato Famine in1845 where such a mass exodus of people from Ireland could have spelt doom for those who opted to travel. There was no guarantee that there would be any jobs or opportunities for them to take advantage of after they arrived. However, with some success stories emerging from this period, most notably that of Andrew Carnegie, it became clear that at least some Irish had found opportunities to find their fortune in America.

There is disagreement over exactly how many Irish immigrated to America during this period, although it is generally accepted that the number was around 2 million. By comparison, Ireland in 1845 was only just recovering from the Great Famine, and it would be fair to say that the vast majority of Irish had no choice but to leave their country. There was also a great deal of political unrest in Ireland during this time and many people expressed concern that they would be forced out of their native land.

This period of mass migration provided an opportunity for some Irish at least to escape the negative treatment they were facing in their own country. However, migration was not without consequences. In the period following the mass migration, employment rates were low, and competition for jobs was high, which meant that wages fell. This was not great for the immigrants who had left Ireland with little money dreaming of a good life in America. Even though there were more opportunities in America, Irish immigrants had to contend with the significant dangers presented by life there. In particular, there were frequent issues relating to their religion and their place in American society as a whole. There were multiple attempts to ban Catholicism in America and it was only in the late 1870s that Irish citizens would be permitted to become American citizens.

Despite all these struggles, some Irish people have gone on to achieve great things in America.

John Fitzgerald Kennedy, the 35th President of the United States is a huge symbol of Irish success in America. Kennedy was born to an elite Irish Catholic family and attended Harvard University eventually becoming a senator for Massachusetts before his career as President. He made history by being the first Catholic President, proving that an Irish person could succeed in America. The Irish had particular success in American politics, something that was not seen with many other races. This has left many to believe that the Irish are 'luckier' than other races living in America.

I do believe the Irish way of life, their cheery dance, the wonderful celebrations of their national holidays, their amazing sense of humour and extreme pride for their country and their outlook on life despite a harsh climate all contribute to their sense of good luck. Their cheerful spirit is contagious and infectious, and you can't help but feel happy and fortunate by being in magical Ireland or in the company of an Irish soul anywhere in the world.

Chapter 8

Luck And Constellations Of Stars

Luck And Constellations Of Stars

During my research, I came to discover a very clear and visible connection between luck, a person's birth month, and a person's star constellations. Indeed, there is a link between perceived luck and your month of birth according to a report from the Edinburgh Science Festival. A summer-winter divide suggests that people born between March and August consider themselves luckier than those born between September and February. May was found to be the luckiest month and October the unluckiest.[1]

People born in May are usually conceived in August, throughout the summer the mother was likely to eat more fresh fruits and vegetables and get more exercise, thus boosting the baby's immune system compared to a winter baby. But what about those born in the Southern Hemisphere where spring begins on the 1st of September, summer on the 1st of December, autumn on the 1st of March, and winter on the 1st of June? Those born between March and August (autumn and winter) would be expected to consider themselves less lucky than those born from September until February (spring and summer) if the season is a causative factor.

According to Mariam Webster's dictionary definition of astrology, it can be defined as "the divination of the supposed influences of the stars and planets on human affairs and terrestrial events by their positions and aspects." This definition is separate from the dictionary definition of astronomy, which is "the study of objects and matter outside the earth's atmosphere."

Back in the days of ancient Babylon, the words "astrology" and "astronomy" meant the same thing but in our modern world, they are defined as two completely different things. In modern times, astrology is viewed with a healthy degree of scepticism and it is considered by many to be a kind of "pseudo-science" that is devoid of any actual scientific principles. There also aren't any respected academics studying in the field of astrology. However, you can easily find professors who are conducting intense research in the fields of astronomy and astrophysics.

Despite this, there are at least some academically minded people that are studying the phenomenon of stars, lucky stars, birth month, zodiac sign, and their possible effects on long-term success in life. In this chapter, we will look at some studies that tried to establish a connection between birth month (as a Chief Executive Officer) and ultimate success later in life. Then we will examine the different zodiac constellations and their impact on our success.

The months of success

Approximately 2,500 years ago, Hippocrates, long considered to be the father of Western Medicine, believed that the movement of celestial bodies in the heavens had a major impact on people's health. While astrology has since been labelled a pseudoscience, that hasn't stopped academics worldwide from conducting studies relating to one's date and month of birth and their prospects in life, both personally and professionally.

The first study we are going to look at began back in 1992 and continued until 2009. In this study, researchers at the University of British Columbia looked at 375 top CEOs of S & P 500 companies and found that only 6.1% of them were born in June and only 5.9% of them were born in July! However, 12.5% of these CEOs had birthdays in March, while 10.7% had birthdays in April. Add those two numbers together, and you get 12% of these CEOs born in the summer vs. 23.2% born in the springtime. This is indeed a very significant find. There was double the number of CEOs who had a springtime birthday vs. a summer birthday.

Non-Astrological Explanation(s)

The professors conducting the above study were not prepared to concede that "luck" and birth month were the actual cause of a CEO's eventual success. The researchers were in search of a more 'logical' explanation for their findings. The researchers suggested that the reason for the significant differences in success between summer and springtime babies has to do with the 'birthday effect'!

The birthday effects

It refers to the cut-off dates established by teachers and institutions of learning for admission to different grade levels in school. For example, in any given class in high school (in North America), you usually find that the kids with springtime

211

birthdays are the older students in the class while the kids with summertime birthdays are the youngest in the class. One of the study's co-authors, Maurice Levi, professor of international finance at the University of British Columbia said in a university press release, "Our findings indicate that summer babies underperform in the ranks of CEOs as a result of the 'birth-date effect,' a phenomenon resulting from the way children are grouped by age in school."

Levi continued by saying, "Older children within the same grade tend to do better than the youngest, who are less intellectually developed. Early success is often rewarded with leadership roles and enriched learning opportunities, leading to future advantages that are magnified throughout life."

He concluded, "We could be excluding some of the business world's best talent simply by enrolling them in school too early." And there you have it - the idea of "luck" was not even acknowledged in this study or even suggested by any researchers. The presumption was that there was no way any of these findings could be as a result of anything other than a simple, no-nonsense, common-sense reason. But should that come as a surprise to us? Certainly not.

The study concluded by stating that although the findings were quite significant, the study could not establish any cause-and-effect relationship. Can it be that such a small age gap can cause so much of a difference in the success rates of students later in life? Are the younger students in the class at that much of a disadvantage by supposedly being enrolled in their classes at "too young" of an age? It does, admittedly, give us pause

212

when we think about it, although further research needs to be done to establish any kind of "cause & effect" relationship.

This study is by no means the only study that pertains to the notions of "luck," "lucky month," or "lucky stars". But since we are talking about CEOs and therefore "professions" and the correlation they may have with your birth month, it would be very fitting to examine another study out of the UK by the Office for National Statistics.

According to their research, children born in December have a higher likelihood of becoming a dentist, while a child born in January is more likely to become a debt collector. Children born in December had a higher probability of becoming an artist, while March babies tended to become pilots later on in life. April, unlike other months, and according to the data, does not have one particular profession linked to it. According to the Office for National Statistics, babies born in April tend to end up in a whole variety of different professions later on in life. They do not tend to follow one career path or another.

A University of Exeter study concluded that most first-time moms in the United States would prefer to have a baby in the springtime. Spring is supposed to be a time of renewal and re-birth; Jesus was said to rise from the dead at Easter, in springtime. The study also concluded that first-time moms would be willing to part with $877 to have their baby born in the springtime.

Another rite of passage, and indeed a milestone in life (along with choosing a career) is getting married, and according to some research, couples that are married in the last 10 days of April tend to have fulfilling marriages full of spontaneity and a "taste for the finer things in life".

April, the magical month

Research[2] has shown that people born in April are healthier than their peers, and also more optimistic. They excel at many jobs and have solid marriages. Both the daisy and the sweet pea are considered birth flowers for April and both of these are imbued with happy feelings: the sweet pea signifies bliss and pleasure, while daisies are said to represent childhood innocence, loyalty and purity. April's babies are extra lucky when it comes to birthstones, with the diamond being known for longevity, strength, beauty and happiness. It is also the most durable of all the birthstones. According to the authors of the Love Zodiac, people who get married under the Aries sign (between April 1 and April 19) are likely to thrive as individuals and have a marriage filled with spontaneity.

According to a Columbia University medical study, people born in April are less likely to be affected by cardiovascular, neurological, respiratory and reproductive diseases than people born throughout the rest of the year. They also score high on what's called the hyperthymia scale, according to U.K. researchers. Hyperthymia is the scientific term for general optimism, so April's babies are likely to see the glass as half-full or to find the silver lining in every situation.

Your health and month of birth

According to researcher David Phillips at the University of Southampton in the UK, babies born from January to March tend to have a higher rate of obesity among males. In one of his studies, Phillips looked at the height and weight data for 1,750 seniors living in England, and he found that 13.8% of men born in winter are considered obese but men born in October to December only had a 9.4% rate of obesity. Women, on the other hand, did not show any measurable differences in obesity rates year-round.

David Phillips hypothesized that babies born in the wintertime were more pre-disposed to obesity in adulthood, as babies born in lower temperatures tend to develop more fatty tissue early on in life. His laboratory work with rats confirmed his hypothesis. Rats that were exposed to cold shortly after birth managed to store more energy as fat.

Temperament

A study conducted in 2004 with 448 men and women aged 20 to 45 and born during the winter months concluded that these men and women tended to resist monotony and engage in more daring activities like going skydiving instead of playing cards. However, once people started progressing into their 50's and beyond, this trend reversed itself, and those older than 45 who were born in summer, preferred the more novelty-seeking activities.

Psychologist Lars-Göran Nilsson of Stockholm University[3] says, "Season of birth does influence temperament;

we just don't know exactly why." He hypothesizes that it has something to do with levels of serotonin and dopamine in the body which influence the formation of personality. He goes on to say that, "Throughout the year, their production fluctuates in a mother's body and might affect the development of a foetus."

Disease and illness

Schizophrenia has a general prevalence of 1% in human beings overall. However, your chances of developing this serious mental illness go up significantly for those born in the winter [4]. This phenomenon has been studied over 200 times in separate studies dating back to 1929. One more recent study published in the New England Journal of Medicine concluded that in the northern hemisphere, people born in March were 11% more likely to develop Schizophrenia than if they were born in June or December. Oddly enough, this trend was reversed in people living in the southern hemisphere. One possible explanation for all this is that these results are directly attributable to prenatal infections like the flu or epidemics like polio, diphtheria, and rubella. People born in August and September were least likely to develop Schizophrenia.

Anthropologist Gerhard Weber of the University of Vienna conducted a study of half a million men in the Austrian National Army and concluded that people born in the spring were on average about 0.2 inches taller than their compatriots who were born in the fall, in fact, October was the birth month of the shortest men in the army. Despite this seemingly small height difference (it would seem), the journal Nature concluded that it was statistically significant. One possible explanation for the height difference could be attributable to melatonin levels found in the mother that stimulates growth hormones.

Multiple Sclerosis (MS), an inflammatory disease, seems more prevalent in babies born in the spring. Also, studies show that the higher the latitude, the higher the risk of developing this serious chronic illness. For example, when it comes to birthdays at specific times of the year, one study of 17,874 Canadians and 11 502 Brits found a 23% greater likelihood of developing MS for those born in May than November. The suspected cause? A decrease in Vitamin D levels in the mother during the second and the third trimester of pregnancy.

Researchers at the University of Bologna in Italy found that summer babies tend to be night owls compared to their winter counterparts. According to their research, people born in August go to bed 19 minutes later on average, than those born in December. According to researcher Vincenzo Natale, our biological circadian rhythms are more or less set in stone the moment we are born. People born in summer are born with a circadian clock that is used to longer days. Early experiments on mice have backed up these claims.

Babies born in the summertime also tend to be left-handed. In a 1994 study in the Journal of Perceptual and Motor Skills, 41.2 % of people born in the summer were left-handed compared to only 38.2% that were right-handed. As of right now, researchers are not exactly sure why, but possible explanations include temperature variations, variation in maternal nutrition depending on the season, and seasonal infections and illnesses like the flu.

Research has shown that summer babies, especially those born in August, are at a higher risk of developing type I Diabetes. In 1999, a Swedish study of 1,248 children with diabetes, found that 24 more babies than expected were born in August while 33 fewer babies were born in October and it is hypothesized that this has something to do with viral infections earlier on in the year that affects the immune system.

Being born in Sweden, for example, increases your risk of developing type 1 diabetes, according to a natural experiment study of children migrating to Sweden.[5]

Babies that were born in the fall months have a higher likelihood of living longer lives. A study of 1,574 people who lived to 100 years and beyond in the US found that relatives of these centenarians who were born in the fall had a 30-50% greater chance of living to 100 and beyond than those relatives that were born in March. Leonoid Gavrilove, who conducted the study along with his wife Natalia at the University of Chicago, suspects (yet again) that possible explanations might have to do with temperatures, Vitamin D exposure, and the prevalence of viral infections!

Japanese, Scandinavian and Dutch studies have all concluded that children are at greater risk of developing allergies if they were born in the fall or winter months. Dr Millo Vassello, a renowned allergy expert at the University Of New York, studied 1000 patients at emergency rooms in Boston who had severe allergic reactions to food. He concluded that people born in the fall and the winter have a 53% higher likelihood of developing an allergy. He suspects that this increase has to do with maternal Vitamin D levels during pregnancy as well as location (for example, far north in the hemisphere).

Mary Regina Boland, Nicholas Tatonetti and other researchers at the Columbia University Department of Medicine examined records for an incredible 1.75 million patients born between 1900 and 2000, who had been treated at Columbia University Medical Centre. Using statistical analysis, they combed through 1,688 different diseases and found 55 that correlated with birth month, including ADHD, reproductive performance, asthma, eyesight and ear infections.[6]

Starry superstitions

Now that we have looked at current studies linking month and season of birth with things like career and health outcomes, let us look at some general superstitions regarding the stars and how they supposedly affect other parts of our lives.

Superstitions surrounding the stars say that you should never count stars as it will bring you bad luck. However, there is one notable exception to this rule: if you are a single person looking for "the one". Folklore would tell you to be careful, though, on this one. There are specific counting rules in place for single, unmarried people. First of all, you can only count to a maximum of seven stars. Second of all, you must do it for seven nights consecutively and then, on the eighth day, the first person of the opposite sex you shake hands with will be the person you marry. Many folklores, however, has it that you should not count any stars at all as it will bring you bad luck. In fact, one legend has it that if you count the stars and reach

100, you will die. There is some debate as to the exact origins of this folklore myth. Some argue that it comes from ancient peoples who worshipped the sun, stars, and the moon, while others argue that this is a more recent superstition.

Rain, luck and agriculture

Legend has it that you can predict upcoming rainfall by looking at the moon. First, check to see if you can see a ring around the moon. Then check the inside of the ring, between the moon and the ring, and count how many stars there are. If you only see one star, it means clear weather is ahead. If you see more than one star, each star represents a day of rain to come. If you saw five stars, it would mean five rainy days for the week. Some cultures consider the stars to represent hours, if you see seven stars, it means seven hours of rain are to come.

For thousands of years, farmers worldwide have used the stars in the heavens to predict the health of their crops. Ancient folklore that can be traced back to England says that if the evening star is low on the horizon, there will be a lousy yield for crops, and if Sirius, the Dog Star is shining brightly, it is said that drought is soon to come.

The predictor of rainfall lies at the heart of the constellation Cancer, which is a cluster of stars resembling a beehive. If it is night-time and the sky is clear, but the "beehive" of Cancer looks faded and hard to see, it is said that rain is on its way. Of course, a logical explanation for star brightness has to do with light pollution, among other things, so if you are near any form of light, your ability to make out certain stars in the night sky can be impaired.

Shooting stars occur randomly and involve no action on our part. They are often very bright flashes of light that can be seen even in severe light pollution. As legend has it, if a shooting star streaks through the sky on your right-hand side, it means good luck is to come. If, however, a shooting star passes off to your left, then you are in for some bad luck. Now, if you are quick on your feet, you can pivot from left to right before the shooting star burns out. If you can do so successfully, you can change bad luck into good luck. Other folklore superstitions that involve shooting stars say that the mere presence of a shooting star in the sky is good luck, but it depends on the person and the circumstances involved. In England, a falling star can represent the soul of a newly born baby ready to begin a new life. It can also mean the soul of a person being released from purgatory to make their way to heaven to find peace. Either way, just the presence of a shooting star in the sky should indicate good luck.

Starlight, star bright

We have all heard the famous nursery rhyme before, perhaps your mother even sang it to you. Did you know that this nursery has its origins in folklore? Stars don't have to be "shooting" to give you good or bad luck. Ancient superstitions in England say that if you pay attention to the heavens when it first gets dark, you can make a wish on the first shining star that you see. If you do, you will get all that your heart desires.

Some versions of this superstition require that you recite a poem or nursery rhyme as you focus on making a wish.

Forbidden to point

We have all heard our parents or grandparents say that it is rude to point but according to legend it also rings true for stars. In ancient times stars were seen as real gods in the sky that were simply taking some time to peer down at us human beings. Therefore, it is been thought that pointing at the stars is just as rude as an individual pointing at another individual. Pointing at a star in some places is considered so bad that if you do so, you can risk bringing bad luck upon you and your family, and it can even lead to your death. So, use your eyes only, and for heaven's sake, don't point!

The Chinese Zodiac

The Chinese zodiac is a classification system based on the lunar calendar that assigns an animal and its reputed attributes to each year in a repeating 12-year cycle. The reason I want to explore the Chinese Zodiac is for the immense importance it has on the perception of luck in Chinese culture. Generally speaking, each astrological sign is part of the astrological wheel and each is said to have certain flaws. They are ostensibly supposed to be learning from each other's signs as we move around the astrological wheel. The zodiac, however, is considered to be a western model of the celestial heavens and if you turn your gaze to the east, you will discover another set of astrological signs that at times, can be a little more explicit when it comes to the negative. For example, if you were born in the year of the goat, it is said that you are destined for bad luck in your life. While many people think these signs are purely superstitious, it does have a profound effect on Chinese society and culture.

The 12 signs of the Chinese zodiac rotate once every 12 years. While some signs are said to give you bad luck (like the goat we mentioned above) there are five stars signs that you could call "lucky stars" as they are said to bring good fortune.

The 12 signs of the Chinese zodiac are Rat, Ox, Tiger, Rabbit, Dragon, Snake, Horse, Goat, Monkey, Rooster, Dog, and Pig. The top five "lucky" signs are Dragon, Snake, Pig, Rat, and Tiger. The most notable of all is the Dragon because it is the sole imaginary animal.

The Year of the Dragon[7]

Years of the Dragon: 1928, 1940, 1952, 1964, 1976, 1988, 2000, 2012, 2024, 2036 and 2048.

The Dragon is the fifth of the 12 Chinese zodiac animals. The Dragon symbolizes power, nobleness, honour, luck, and success in traditional Chinese culture. The Dragon is a supernatural being with no parallel for talent and excellence. Among the Chinese zodiac animals, the dragon is the most vital and powerful beast in the Chinese zodiac, even though Dragons have an infamous reputation for being hot-headed and possessing a sharp tongue. In ancient times, people thought that Dragons were best suited to be the leaders of the world with their dominance and ambition.

People who are born in the year of the dragon will grow up to become natural-born leaders. They are ambitious and very knowledgeable and many Chinese people do believe that people that are born in the year of the dragon are indeed descendants of dragons. They are creative but also mysterious and they set strict goals for themselves and their subordinates. Dragons can sometimes be harsh and abrupt with the people that work under them and they have a tendency to berate others when they believe their orders are not being followed properly.

The year 2020 was a year of the rat. People born in this year are said to be destined for good luck. Career-wise they will likely do well and earn all the degrees and certifications required for their careers. Those born in the year of the rat are said to be generally healthy, with possibilities for respiratory diseases. Does the Covid-19 pandemic ring any bells here?

Although astrology as a whole has been dismissed by astronomers and scientists alike, the Chinese zodiac appears to have a much deeper meaning for modern-day society in the East than the Western zodiac has for inhabitants of western countries. The Chinese zodiac has also had a heavy influence on the zodiacs of other eastern nations like Vietnam, the Koreas, Myanmar, Japan, Thailand and Burma. Have a look at the zodiac signs for each of these countries:

> Japan: Rat, Ox, Tiger, Rabbit, Dragon, Snake, Horse, Goat, Monkey, Rooster, Dog, and Boar

> Vietnam: Rat, Buffalo, Tiger, Cat, Dragon, Snake, Horse, Goat, Monkey, Rooster, Dog, and Pig

➢ Thailand: Rat, Ox, Tiger, Rabbit, Naga (a mythical half-human-half-snake spirit), Snake, Horse, Goat, Monkey, Rooster, Dog, and Pig

➢ Burma: Garuda (a mythical bird), Tiger, Lion, Elephant (with tusks), Rat, Guinea Pig, and Dragon

Japanese lucky stars of love

There is a Japanese mythical legend involving love that has been passed down from one generation to the next. A young girl named Hoshi loved the stars, so she would lie down in the soft grass at night, watching the stars. They transfixed her, and she would go out to lie underneath the stars every single night. One night she noticed that some stars had begun falling, and she became worried that these stars would disappear forever. The next night, after having first observed the shooting stars, she noticed that there were now fewer stars in the sky. She decided that if she were to make origami stars out of paper and then place them in a jar, it would bring good luck in love to whomever she gifted the jar of stars to. So, she ran from house to house, knocking on every door and encouraged all of her family to come to make lucky stars with her. They began making different stars in all kinds of quantities and putting them in jars to give away as gifts. The meaning of the number of stars in a given jar is as follows:

1 star: The only love

2 stars: The happy and compatible couple

30 stars: Love for a lifetime

55 stars: Love you without regret

99 stars: May the friendship/love last forever

101 stars: You are the only one in my life

129 stars: The border-less love

365 stars: A whole year of blessings

548 stars: Wishing you would love me endlessly

999 stars: Everlasting love

1314 stars: Eternal love

Lucky stars, astrology and modern physics

If you will recall earlier in the chapter, we looked at numerous studies of people born in certain months and how they fared later in life (according to statistical data) both from a standpoint of success in their careers, but also in matters related to health or simple things like height. All of these studies used sound statistical data, and as you can expect, that is not what scientists have taken issue with over the years. Researchers have sought to explain all of these differences in the zodiac with numerous theories ranging from everything like levels of maternal vitamin D in the month of birth to things like certain monthly variations in growth hormone levels (explaining differences in height) and what hemisphere you were born in.

Scientists, in general, are not likely to give any credence to theories (that explain these statistical variations) that have anything to do with notions of luck or perceived mysticism. Indeed, as you will recall, astrology was long ago labelled a pseudoscience and separated from the studies of astronomy, physics, and even western medicine. But if we look at modern-day science, there is room to ask questions about things that could be considered mythical or spiritual.

As one scientist puts it, if the nucleus of a cell was the size of an apple, the next closest particle would be the size of a grain of salt and located approximately 1 km away. We all seem to be physical beings yet at the core of our cells, there are simply empty spaces of energy.

For a long time, western astronomy, physics and medicine treated the body as if it were just a machine with different levers, pulleys, and screws that just needed tightening and adjusting from time to time. In 1925, a new physics emerged called quantum physics, and from Steven Hawking to your local college professor, everyone can agree that quantum physics is a legitimate science that no one fully understands. So, without diving into complex mathematical equations, quantum physics at its most basic level says that there are waves of energy all around us that are vibrating in what is known as the quantum field.

Not long before he died, Steven Hawking and his team were still trying to figure out how black holes worked and the laws of physics that governed them. Today, we still don't have all the answers. If there are unknown, invisible forces of energy that are affecting the physical realm does that not sound like the whole religious concept of "spirit". At its most basic level, the idea of spirit revolves around mysterious forces that shape our world.

So, while there are good reasons scientists can use to reject the notions of lucky stars, or mythology, or astrology, does it not give you pause that we now also have a widely accepted branch of physics that says we don't understand all the invisible forces of energy around us and how they impact our material world. Can't some of these invisible forces be the luck we seek so desperately all our life?

Chapter 9

Quotes About Luck

Quotes About Luck

Throughout history, luck has never ceased to fascinate humans. The rich and famous, leaders and presidents, even kings and emperors all consulted fortune-tellers and wizards for luck and good fortune. In this chapter, I chose to include some interesting quotes about luck. These quotes give us a different yet interesting and sometimes amusing understanding of luck lived through deeply meaningful life experiences. I saw it fitting to include them in this book because by examining these words, we can gain a deeper understanding of the essence of luck from a historical and current personal perspective.

I would like to thank good reads and brainy quotes for making some of them available.

Quotes

'' Throw a lucky man in the sea and he will survive and come up with a fish in his mouth''

— Arab proverb

'' Luck sometimes visits a fool, but never sits down with him ''

— German Proverb

'' When your luck deserts you, even cold food burns ''

— African Proverb

''The latitude and longitudinal lines of where you are born determine your opportunity in life, and it's not equal. We may have been created equal, but we're not born equal. It's a lot to do with luck and you have to pass that on.''

— Brad Pitt

''The year 1999, seventh month, from Heaven will come a great king of terror: to bring back to life the great King of Angolmois. Before and after Mars to reign by good luck.''

— Nostradamus

'' I have had bad luck with all my wives. The first one left me and the second one didn't. The third gave me more children! ''

—Donald Trump

"Remember that sometimes not getting what you want is a wonderful stroke of luck."

— Dalai Lama XIV

''It was the nation and the race dwelling all around the globe that had the lion's heart. I had the luck to be called upon to give the roar.''

—Winston Churchill

"I think we consider too much the luck of the early bird and not enough the bad luck of the early worm."

— Franklin D. Roosevelt

'' The only thing you have to worry about is bad luck. I never had bad luck''

— Harry S. Truman

"I'm a greater believer in luck, and I find the harder I work the more I have of it"

— Thomas Jefferson

''There are two types of poor people, those who are poor together and those who are poor alone. The first are the true poor, the others are rich people out of luck.''

— Jean-Paul Sartre

''Some people, through luck and skill, end up with a lot of assets. If you're good at kicking a ball, writing software, investing in stocks, it pays extremely well.''

— Bill Gates

''Luck and being honest and sincere about work has worked for me and helped me reach where I am.''

— Katrina Kaif

''As an actor I am always waiting for my luck to run out.''

— Tom Hanks

"People say they don't believe in luck: luck is the reason the dinosaurs got wiped out and why human beings became the new dominant species on this planet."

— Stewart Stafford

''Look, sometimes, no matter how hard you try, sometimes you need a bit of luck.''

— Bear Grylls

''I may have had a lot of luck in my life, but I still need to find a challenge in the game.''

—Zinedine Zidane

''People often remark that I'm pretty lucky. Luck is only important in so far as getting the chance to sell yourself at the right moment. After that, you've got to have talent and know how to use it.''

— Frank Sinatra

"Luck enters into every contingency. You are a fool if you forget it -- and a greater fool if you count upon it."

— Phyllis Bottome

''For a long time now, I have tried simply to write the best I can. Sometimes I have good luck and write better than I can.''

— Ernest Hemingway

"Good luck is more dangerous than bad luck. Bad luck teaches valuable lessons about patience, timing, and the need to be prepared for the worst; good luck deludes you into the opposite lesson, making you think your brilliance will carry you through. Your fortune will inevitably turn, and when it does you will be completely unprepared."

— Robert Greene, The 48 Laws of Power

''Luck is a strong horse; it can carry man to very distant places!''

— Mehmet Murat ildan

"Patience's design flaw became obvious for the first time in my life: the outcome is decided not during the course of play but when the cards are shuffled, before the game even begins. How pointless is that?"

— David Mitchell, Cloud Atlas

"One chance is enough for a winner."

— Ankit Devanshi

''The brave men die in war. It takes great luck or judgment not to be killed. Once, at least, the head has to bow and the knee has to bend to danger. The soldiers who march back under the triumphal arches are death's deserters.''

— Jean Giraudoux

"If grace belongs to God, there are those who say that luck belongs to the Devil and that he looks after his own."

— Sarah Dunant, In the Company of the Courtesan

"Fate would have it that the timing of your birth determines your measure of luck. You are either born lucky or you are not, though the only way to know for sure is to test it. The problem with that is most people find out they are not lucky at the worst possible moment, usually in the throes of death or arrest."

— Tanya Thompson, Red Russia

"My father had always told me that sea birds were the souls of lost traders. To turn them away or not give them a place to land or nest was bad luck."

— Adrienne Young, Fable

"Some call it fate, some call it luck, some call it accident, some call it coincidence, some call it an answer to prayers, I call it karma."

— Rupa Mahanti, Thoughts: A Collection of Inspirational Quotes

"No one I met at this time -- doctors, nurses, practicians, or fellow-patients-- failed to assure me that a man who is hit through the neck and survives it is the luckiest creature alive. I could not help thinking that it would be even luckier not to be hit at all."

— George Orwell, Homage to Catalonia

"Luck is a goddess not to be coerced and forcibly wooed by those who seek her favours. From such masterful spirits she turns away. But it happens sometimes that, if we put our hand in hers with the humble trust of a little child, she will have pity on us, and not fail us in our hour of need."

— P.G. Wodehouse

'' A great man's greatest good luck is to die at the right time ''

— Eric Hoffer

'' You never know what worse luck your bad luck has saved you from."

— Cormac McCarthy, No Country for Old Men

"Shallow men believe in luck or in circumstance. Strong men believe in cause and effect."

— Ralph Waldo Emerson

"If I could, I'd write a huge encyclopedia just about the words luck and coincidence"

— Paulo Coelho, The Alchemist

"The sun doesn't just hang on one family's tree"

— Anchee Min, Empress Orchid

"Oh, but you must travel through those woods again and again... said a shadow at the window... and you must be lucky to avoid the wolf every time...But the wolf... the wolf only needs enough luck to find you once."

— Emily Carroll, Through the Woods

''Most of us regard good luck as our right, and bad luck as a betrayal of that right. ''

— William Feather

"Luck has a way of evaporating when you lean on it."

— Brandon Mull, Keys to the Demon Prison

"Lucky people should hide. Pray the days of wrath do not visit their home."

— Josephine Hart, Damage

"It takes only a split second for life to go horribly wrong. To fix the mess, I need a thousand things to go right. The distance from one bit of luck to the next feels as great as the distance across oceans. But I decide in this moment, I will bridge that distance, again and again, until I win. I will not fail."

— Sabaa Tahir, A Torch Against the Night

"Luck is the residue of design."

— John Milton

"With a library it is easier to hope for serendipity than to look for a precise answer."

— Lemony Snicket, When Did You See Her Last?

"I've found that what most people call luck is often little more than raw talent combined with the ability to make the most of opportunities. (Talon Karrde)"

— Timothy Zahn, Heir to the Empire

"Luck is a word the bitter teaches to the ignorant."

— Steve Maraboli, Unapologetically You: Reflections on Life and the Human Experience

"Trust your luck, Taran Wanderer. But don't forget to put out your nets!"

— Lloyd Alexander, Taran Wanderer

"Lightning doesn't strike twice."

— Robert Galbraith, The Silkworm

"There are rules to luck, not everything is chance for the wise; luck can be helped by skill."

— Balthasar Gracian, The Art of Worldly Wisdom

"Plus, he was naturally lucky at cards. As Mam had always said, lucky at cards, or lucky at life. One or the other. Not both."

— Cinda Williams Chima, The Exiled Queen

"Luck is not as random as you think. Before that lottery ticket won the jackpot, someone had to buy it."

— Vera Nazarian, The Perpetual Calendar of Inspiration

"Learn to recognize good luck when it's waving at you, hoping to get your attention."

— Sally Koslow

"You know, if you are an American and you are born at this time in history especially, you are lucky. We all are. We won the world history Powerball lottery."

— Bill Maher

''Richard Burton came from the same town as me, so I thought I'd follow my nose, and follow my luck. I think I've been very lucky.''

—Anthony Hopkins

"I may say that this is the greatest factor: the way in which the expedition is equipped, the way in which every difficulty is foreseen, and precautions taken for meeting or avoiding it. Victory awaits him who has everything in order, luck, people call it. Defeat is certain for him who has neglected to take the necessary precautions in time, this is called bad luck."

— Roald Amundsen

"I do strongly feel that among the greatest pieces of luck for high achievement is ordeal. Certain great artists can make out without it, Titian and others, but mostly you need ordeal. My idea is this: the artist is extremely lucky who is presented with the worst possible ordeal which will not actually kill him. At that point, he's in business: Beethoven's deafness, Goya's deafness, Milton's blindness, that kind of thing."

— John Berryman

"...luck is not to be coerced."

— Albert Camus

"Luck which so often defies anticipation in matrimonial affairs, giving attraction to what is moderate rather than to what is superior."

— Jane Austen, Emma

"Together they spent their whole lives waiting for their luck to change, as though luck were some fabulous tides that would one day flood and consecrate the marshes of our island, christening us in the iridescent ointments of a charmed destiny."

— Pat Conroy, The Prince of Tides

"I'm one of those who doesn't think there is much difference between an atomic scientist and a man who cleans the crappers except for the luck of the draw - parents with enough money to point you toward a more generous death. of course, some come through brilliantly, but there are thousands, millions of others, bottled up, kept from even the most minute chance to realize their potential."

— Charles Bukowski

"Some call it fate, some call it luck, some call it accident, some call it coincidence, some call it an answer to prayers, I call it karma."

— Rupa Mahanti, Thoughts: A Collection of Inspirational Quotes

"If it is too good to be true then it is a trap, god blesses no one with these much luck."

— Sarvesh Jain

"If you have a bad luck at the dawn, you had a bad luck. If you keep having bad luck all day, you are the bad luck."

— Amit Kalantri, Wealth of Words

"You can spoil your good luck with your stupidity, but even with all the smartness in the world, you can never outrun your bad luck."

— Shon Mehta, Stories of Jivavarta

"For our success to happen, millions of billions of things, the vast majority of which were neither in our control nor in our awareness, needed not only to happen but also to happen how, when, where, and—in some cases—for how long, they have happened; and to happen to the things and the people to whom they have happened."

— Mokokoma Mokhonoana, On Friendship: A Satirical Essay

"In a sea of a thousand mines, the crew of the Life maker had to be lucky a thousand times, but in that same sea, the Regime only had to be lucky once."

— Dean F. Wilson, Lifemaker

"Pearls were accidents, and the finding of one was luck, a little pat on the back by God or the gods or both."

— John Steinbeck, The Pearl

"Be bold. Be brave. Don't thank your lucky stars. The stars can't hear you."

— Felix Dennis

"Every victory or defeat is always partly a matter of luck..."

— Tamuna Tsertsvadze, Gift of the Fox

"Luck will do nothing for you if you're not consistently earning the right to receive it."

— Oscar Auliq-Ice

"Luck is a finite and rare substance in the universe, like palladium or cobalt. To use it, you have to take it from somebody else."

— Catherynne M. Valente, The Refrigerator Monologues

"Never knew if you had any luck left unless you pushed it."

— James S.A. Corey, Leviathan Wakes

"Luck does favour the prepared"

— James Stoakes, Power: Awakening

"Luck, of course, will always play a role, as it does with all strategies"

— W. Chan Kim, Blue Ocean Strategy

"Only the way is, one can pray to change its luck, but one cannot fight its luck."

— Ehsan Sehgal

"I've always believed in luck. I love the fact that people can change their lives instantly."

— Fiona Barton, The Widow

"Luck is my middle name," said Rincewind, indistinctly. "Mind you, my first name is Bad."

— Terry Pratchett

"Marry on Monday for health, Tuesday for wealth, Wednesday the best day of all, Thursday for crosses, Friday for losses, and Saturday for no luck at all."

— Folk Rhyme

"Luck is blind, they say. It can't see where it's going and keeps running into people...and the people it knocks into we call lucky! Well, to hell with luck if it's like that, I say!"

— Nikos Kazantzakis, Zorba the Greek

"Our life is our only chance..."

— Laure Lacornette

"The best luck always happens to people who don't need it."

— Robert Penn Warren, All the King's Men

"But bad luck makes good stories."

— Bernard Evslin

"It is not very often that an opportunity comes knocking. But when it does, you better be bathed and dressed and ready to answer its call."

— Jyoti Arora, Dream's Sake

"They claimed no allegiance to any flag and valued no currency but luck and good contacts."

— Hunter S. Thompson, The Rum Diary

"While persistence offers no guarantees, it does give 'luck' a chance to operate."

— Tom Shippey, The Road to Middle-Earth: How J.R.R. Tolkien Created a New Mythology

'' I agree with Sophocles: the greatest luck is not to have been born - but, as the joke goes on, very few people succeed in it. ''

— Slavoj Zizek

''I busted a mirror and got seven years bad luck, but my lawyer thinks he can get me five.'' — Steven Wright

''Dear World, I am leaving because I am bored. I feel I have lived long enough. I am leaving you with your worries in this sweet cesspool. Good luck. ''

— George Sanders

''I guess if there weren't luck involved, I'd win 'em all. ''

— Phil Hellmuth

''The universe works in crazy ways. Your good luck will come in waves, and so does your bad, so you have to take the good with the bad and press forward.''

— Nick Cummins

''With luck, you have other things to do than wait for lightning to strike. ''

— Paul Lauterbur

''Destiny is a good thing to accept when it's going your way. When it isn't, don't call it destiny; call it injustice, treachery, or simple bad luck.''

— Joseph Heller

''I believe in luck and fate and I believe in karma, that the energy you put out in the world comes back to meet you.''

— Chris Pine

''Success is always a matter of some luck and timing.''

— Kathleen Kennedy

"Captaincy is 90 per cent luck and 10 per cent skill. But don't try it without that 10 per cent."

— Richie Benaud

"It is by universal misunderstanding that all agree. For if, by ill luck, people understood each other, they would never agree."

— Charles Baudelaire

"I don't believe in luck. Not in golf, anyway. There are good bounces and bad bounces, sure, but the ball is round and so is the hole. If you find yourself in a position where you hope for luck to pull you through, you're in serious trouble."

— Jack Nicklaus

"Be grateful for luck. Pay the thunder no mind - listen to the birds. And don't hate nobody."

— Eubie Blake

"Pray for intestinal fortitude, work hard, and keep the faith. Oh, and pray for good luck, you're gonna need it."

— Jerry Reed

"You get rich through luck. You get rich through crime. You get rich through fulfilling the needs of another. You can be as greedy as you like. If you can't do one of those three things, you ain't going to get any money."

—David Mamet

"If you're healthy, if you don't get sick much, if you don't go to the doctor much or use your health insurance much, you are a genetic lottery winner. It has nothing to do with the way you live, nothing to do with doing the right things. It's just sheer luck, and you are gonna pay for that."

—Rush Limbaugh

"Give luck a chance to happen."

—Tom Kite

"Only bad golfers are lucky. They're the ones bouncing balls off trees, curbs, turtles and cars. Good golfers have bad luck. When you hit the ball straight, a funny bounce is bound to be unlucky."

— Lee Trevino

"Being famous is complete luck, and that's something you can't bank on."

— Bo Burnham

"Luck affects everything. Let your hook always be cast; in the stream where you least expect it there will be a fish."

— Ovid

"The only good luck many great men ever had was being born with the ability and determination to overcome bad luck."

— Channing Pollock

"The worst cynicism: a belief in luck."

— Joyce Carol Oates

"Good night, and good luck."

— Edward R. Murrow

"Luck is a very thin wire between survival and disaster, and not many people can keep their balance on it."

— Hunter S. Thompson

"I don't mean to criticize anyone in any way that I wouldn't criticize myself. I think people should have fun, and have a good time, and enjoy the luck that we have to be lazy and dwell in consumerism. But I think that it's a balance. And our job as actors is empathy."

— Natalie Portman

"It is a great piece of skill to know how to guide your luck even while waiting for it."

— Baltasar Gracian

"Sometimes bad luck hits you like in an ancient Greek tragedy, and it's not your own making. When you have a plane crash, it's not your fault."

—Werner Herzog

"We've had bad luck with our kids - they've all grown up."

— Christopher Morley

"Ambition drives you on, ability certainly helps, but the fickle finger of fate and luck are great things."

—Fergus Henderson

''What's happened in my career is probably fate and good luck.''

— Pruitt Taylor Vince

From these rich and beautiful quotes, we can understand how people faced life and navigated the troubled seas that sometimes overwhelm us. For some, luck is real and the main propeller of success, for others, it is all about hard work and a happy mentality. Nevertheless, *luck is there and even those who deny its existence are indeed lucky to be able to deny luck. They did not need it in their lives because they were born lucky.*

My Own Conclusion

Your luck (good or bad) is born with you like your fingerprints, unique to you. It will stay with you for the rest of your life with no escape, although I do believe hard work potentially and only to some extent can make your life better, hard work alone is never enough. Millions of people put so much hard work into a new business, or a promising relationship just to see it crumble in front of their own eyes due to bad luck in the form of events they could not control.

We, humans, are the most complicated of all the creations that have ever existed. Life is the most unpredictable thing that we own, yet our life revolves around fallacies and imaginations that cannot always come true. Luck is true and is all around us but we cannot see it. While we are praying for it and hoping in hard times that there will be light at the end of the tunnel, luck is the tunnel that leads either to light or to more abysmal darkness.

Faced with serious questions while living this life, we should be able to find answers to issues inside ourselves, but I believe the background noise is sometimes so loud that we do not hear our internal guiding voice. We are seduced by external forces to find easy answers, answers that we might just find ourselves if we were determined enough and ready to engage in some serious self-reflection.

Nobody knows the true meaning of life. Maybe one life is not enough to understand what it means to be alive. The fact that we are breathing now means we are lucky to be alive, healthy with a sound mind.

During the Covid-19 pandemic in 2020, which affected our world so badly, more than 97,966 businesses in the USA were permanently shut down according to yelp's local economic impact report. I wonder about the long years of hard work these owners have put in to advance their businesses not knowing that one bad luck event like Covid-19 could destroy all their effort, while the same event was a stroke of good luck for Jeff Bezos, the founder of Amazon, who got his immense fortune to multiply without any additional work. Even starting Amazon, itself was a lucky event. In 1994 Bezos was in NYC working for a hedge fund and by chance, he saw a startling statistic about the coming explosion of web user numbers and he thought about starting amazon. What if Bezos was not working for that specific hedge fund – would he have come across those statistics? Maybe Jeff Bezos was born under a lucky star…. for sure.

I see luck as the engine and your hard work and mentality are just the wheels, if the engine does not start, your wheels will take you nowhere, your hard work and lucky mentality will not make you win the lottery, or avoid cancer! Recent well respected scientific studies have suggested strongly that luck and opportunity play an underappreciated role in determining the ultimate level of individual success, something I have always been convinced of.

Yet science fails to understand how luck works or which laws govern its movements. As on the famous night on August

18, 1913, in Monte Carlo's Le Grande Casino illustrates, luck is indeed bizarre, mysterious and beyond comprehension. On that crazy night, at the roulette wheel, the colour black came up 29 times in a row – that is a 1 in 136,823,184 probability. Massive amounts of money were lost that night, why? After the wheel came up black the tenth time, gamblers began placing more larger bets on the red, on the false assumption that black could not possibly come up again, but it kept coming again and again. What science or natural law can explain this?

Luck as I see it is born with us, you are indeed born lucky or unlucky. Unlike most major religions, which insist luck does not exist and unlike science which is trying to fit luck into a mathematical model, luck in my opinion is a paranormal force that does exist. You can call it the hand of God, or the will of the universe. It is meant to be with you for the good or the bad, we don't know which side we were born under, the lucky or the unlucky and you can't choose not to be born in an unlucky land torn apart by dictators, wars and natural disasters. Luck comes first.

If you feel you are unlucky, you need to completely disown luck from your life, insulate yourself from any situations that require luck, work to make your life more satisfying and deeper in substance, because unlucky people can be happy ones as well. Acceptance is happiness in some way.

When you are faced with episodes of bad luck, the old boring classical quotes about hard work and success does not ring true for me. I believe you must make an effort, work hard and give it your best and hope the winds of luck will blow in your favour. There is always this hidden mysterious force hovering over our lives.

If you feel that you are lucky, then continue to apply your rules and standards of a lucky life. Many lottery winners believed they will win one day. If you have this gut feeling, then never give up, if you feel you will win one day, then play the lottery until your last breath. Persistence increases your luck and you shall win. If you believe you will one day, find your soulmate, then never stop searching even if you got your heart broken many times.

Luck is real and is indeed a major force in our lives, without it, you can never succeed.

"The entire universe is inside you. Stop acting so small. You are the universe in ecstatic motion. Set your life on fire. Seek those who fan your flames."   — Rumi

References

Chapter 1

Luck throughout history

[1-2] Mele, A. R. (2008). Free Will and Luck (1st ed.) Oxford University Press. P 76 – 7. P36-41.

[3] The Old Testament Student, A Babylonian Saints' Calendar, 1887

[4] Yamamoto, Keiji (2007). "Abū Maʿshar Jaʿfar ibn Muḥammad ibn ʿUmar al-Balkhi". In Thomas Hockey; et al. (eds.). The Biographical Encyclopaedia of Astronomers. New York: Springer. p. 11. ISBN 978-0-387-31022-0

[5] Tobsha Learner, Royal Astrologers: How Kings & Queens have used astrologers over the years. Sloan Magazine, February 2019.

Chapter 2

Ovarian Lottery and The Myth of Hard work

[1] N. Taylor Thompson, Life is Luck — Here's How to Plan a Career Around It, Harvard Business Review, January 27, 2014

[2] James Clear, Life Lessons, Blog Article, Accessed May 2021

[3] Rainer Zitelmann, Are Successful People Just 'Luckier' Than Everyone Else? Forbes, Sep 9, 2019.

[4] Robert H. Frank, Quartz, Blog Article, July 21, 2016

[5][6][7][8] Lauren Gray, Beslifeonline, Blog Article, June 14, 2019

[9] Stephen Wagner, liveabout.com, April 18, 2019

[10] Alima Hotakie, how big a role does luck play in football? Aljazeera,13 Jul 2018

[11] Prateek Vasisht, The role of Luck in football? Quantifying the Quirky, totalfootball. Medium.com, March 20, 2019

[12-13] Zoe Beaty, Work Hard & You'll Succeed' Simply Isn't True, So Let's Stop Saying It, refinery29, 12 March 2020

[14] The dirty secret about success, Worklife, BBC, Accessed May 2021

[15] Thomas Waschenfelder, The Myth of Hard Work: It Matters Less Than You Think, wealest.com, Accessed May 2021

Chapter 3

Luck and Religion

[1] Vancouver Sun, The history of luck, Author of the article: Douglas Todd, Publishing date: Mar 17, 2012

[2] Wikipedia. Khvarenah

[3] Wikipedia, Judaism

[4] Judaism and Common Superstitions, Dr. Yvette Alt Miller, Oct 28, 2018 via aish.com

[5] Rabbai Jeremy Rosen, Do Jews Believe in Luck? the Algemeiner, Nov 23, 2012

[6] Professor Ely Merzbach , Using Lotteries in Logic of Halakhah Law. The Meaning of Randomness in Judaism Studia Humana, Volume 6:2 (2017), pp. 107—115, DOI: 10.1515/sh-2017-0014

[7] Prof Ely Merzbach Reuven, The Logic of the Lot: The Significance of the Lottery and Randomness in Judaism, Mass Publishers (Hebrew), 208 pages, NIS 82, Accessed May 2021.

[8] Erik Raymond, thegospelcoalition.org, Blog Article, March 23, 2007

[9] Compellingtruth.org, Blog Article, Accessed May 2021

[10] T. Sean Sullivan, La Vista Church of Christ, February 10, 2021

[11] Al-Quazwini, S.M. (2012)., Discovering Islam website 's archive.Accessed May 2021

[12] Grand Ayatollah Jafar Sobhani, Secrets of Success, Blog Article, al-islam.org, Accessed May 2021

[13] Anand Sagar Pathak, What is Luck? Times of India, Apr 4, 2019

[14] Das, Subhamoy. "Lakshmi: The Hindu Goddess of Wealth and Beauty." Learn Religions, Aug. 27, 2020

[15] Buddha net, Good Luck and Fate, Good Question Good Answer with Ven. S. Dhammika, Accessed May 2021.

[16] Good Luck in Chinese Culture, Asian inspirations website. Accessed May 2021

[17] The Wayback Machine. British Taoist Association, 2006

[18] Chinese good luck symbols". goodlucksymbols.com. Good luck symbols, Accessed May 2021

[19] ChinaKnowledge.de - An Encyclopaedia on Chinese History, Literature and Art & Wikipedia. Accessed May 2021

[20] Chiba, Reiko (1995). The seven lucky gods of Japan.

[21] Reiko, Chiba (1966). The Seven Lucky Gods of Japan. Charles E. Tuttle Co. pp. 9–10.

[22] Charles Q. Choi, Ancient Egyptian Calendar Reveals Earliest Record of 'Demon Star' livescience.com May 31, 2012

[23] Sebastian Porceddu, Lauri Jetsu,Tapio Markkanen & Jaana Toivari-Viitala, Evidence of Periodicity in Ancient Egyptian Calendars of Lucky and Unlucky Days. Cambridge Archaeological Journal 18 (3). DOI:10.1017/S0959774308000395.

Chapter 4

Luck and Fortune-Tellers

[1] Wikipedia, Witchcraft, Accessed June 2021

[2] Merriam Webster blog article, 9 Words from the Magical Realm, Accessed June 2021

[3] Wikidiff, Psychic vs Witch - What's the difference? Accessed June 2021

[4] Diffen, Gecko vs. Lizard, Accessed June 2021

[5] Prelutsky, J. (1983). The random house book of poetry for children. Penguin Random House. ISBN 9780394850108.

[6] Mary Shons, BBC Teach, 21 January 2011

[7] Mary Shons, National Geographic, 21 January 2011

[8] Melanie McGrath, The witching hour, The Guardian, 28 October 2000

[9] Arts and Culture Google, Editorial, Accessed June 2021

[10] Rolling Stones, 1962, Lyrics published on Lyricfind blog, Accessed June 2021

[11] James Valentine and Adam Levine 2012, published on Musixmatch.

[12] WorldAtlas.com, Editorial, Accessed June 2021

[13] Travelchinaguide.com, Accessed June 2021.

[14] Jin Qian, [Cheat Sheet]: Chinese Fortune Telling, smartshanghai.com, 16 July 2015

Chapter 5

Luck and Science

[1] Pluchino, A., Biondo, A. E. & Rapisarda, A. (2018). Talent vs Luck: The Role of Randomness in Success and Failure. Advances in Complex Systems, 21: 03n04.

[2] Wiseman, R. (2003) the luck factor, Miramax Publishing. ISBN 0786869143

[3] Janoff-Bulman, R. (1992). Shattered assumptions: Towards a new psychology of trauma. New York: Free Press

[4] Pritcharda, D. & Smith, M. (2004). The psychology and philosophy of luck. New Ideas in Psychology 21 (1): 1-28. DOI 10.1016/j.newideapsych.2004.03.001.

[5] Levinson, H.C. (2001). Chance, Luck, Statistics: The science of Chance. Dover Publications. ISBN: 0486419975.

[6] Darke, P.R. & Freedman, J.L. (1997). The Belief in Good Luck Scale. Journal of Research and Personality 31, 486–511.

[7] Rotter, J.B. (1955). The role of the psychological situation in determining the direction of human behaviour. The Nebraska Symposium on Motivation 3:245-269.

[8] Darke, P.R. & Freedman, J.L. (1997). The Belief in Good Luck Scale. Journal of Research and Personality.

[9] Dunbar, K., & Fugelsang, J. (2005). Causal thinking in science: How scientists and students interpret the unexpected.

In M. E. Gorman, R. D. Tweney, D. Gooding & A. Kincannon (Eds.), Scientific and Technological Thinking (pp. 57–79). Mahwah, NJ: Lawrence Erlbaum Associates.

[10] Baumeister, A.A. (1976). Serendipity and the cerebral localization of pleasure. Neoplasma. Department of Psychology, Louisiana State University. 23 (3): 259–63. PMID 8738.

[11] Roberts, R. M. (1989). Serendipity: Accidental Discoveries in Science. John Wiley & Sons, Inc. New York.

[12] Gaughan, R. (2010). Accidental Genius: The world's greatest by-chance discoveries. Metro Books. ISBN 978-1-4351-2557-5.

[13] Wikipedia, Luck, Accessed June 2021

[14] Sirkar, S.K. (2010). How to be lucky and successful in life. Pothi.com E Book, p. 5.

[15] Maltby, J., Day, L., Gill, P., Colley, A. & Wood, A.M. (2008). Beliefs around luck: Confirming the empirical conceptualization of beliefs around luck and the development of the Darke and Freedman beliefs around luck scale. Archived 2011-07-17 at the Way back Machine Personality and Individual Differences, 45, 655–660.

[16] Ossola, A., The Science of luck, Popular Science, March 17, 2015.

[17] Barry, S., The role of luck in life success is far greater than we realized, Scientific American, March 1, 2018

Chapter 6

The Lucky Mentality

[1] Depression. World Health Organization, Accessed 30 Jan 2020.

[2] Association for Psychological Science Intuition, It's More Than a Feeling. Retrieved 7 June 2021

[3] Psychology Compass, contradict yourself to become more open-minded, Accessed 3 Feb 2020.

[4] Zhan, L., Guo, D., Chen, G., & Yang, J. (2018). Effects of repetition learning on associative recognition over time: Role of the hippocampus and prefrontal cortex. Frontiers in human neuroscience, 12: 277.

[5] Schmelzer, G., Understanding learning and memory: The neuroscience of repetition. Gretchen Schmelzer. Accessed January, 2015.

[6] Chu, M., This researcher reveals how lucky people differ from unlucky people. Inc, Accessed January 5, 2021.

[7] Lerner, J.S., Li, Y., Valdesolo, P., Kassam, K.S. (2015). Emotion and decision making. Annual Review Psychology 3 (66):799-823. DOI: 10.1146/annurev-psych-010213-115043.

[8] Mayo Clinic, Positive thinking: Stop negative self-talk to reduce stress. Accessed January 21, 2020.

[9] Cascio, C. N., O'Donnell, M. B., Tinney, F. J., Lieberman, M. D., Taylor, S. E., Strecher, V. J., & Falk, E. B. (2016). Self-affirmation activates brain systems associated with self-related processing and reward and is reinforced by future orientation. Social cognitive and affective neuroscience, 11(4): 621–629.

[10] Helpguide, Benefits of mindfulness, a Harvard Health Article. Accessed April, 20, 2021.

[11] Farber, N., These are the 8 habits of highly lucky people. Psychology Today. Accessed July 2021.

Chapter 7

Luck of the Irish

[1] Harry Brent, where does the term 'Luck of the Irish' originate from? Irish Post - 4/10/2019

[2] Warren, C. (2014). Honest liars - The psychology of self-deception, TedX Talk.

[3] O'Donnell, E.T. (2002). 1001 Things everyone should know about Irish history. Break Time Books. ISBN-10: 0767906861.

[4] Osburn, C., Survey on the world's sexiest accents, the knowledge academy, Accessed April 15, 2020

[5] Edwards, R.D. & Williams, T.D. (1957). The Great Famine: Studies in Irish history. New York: New York University Press. pp.517

[6] Woolf, A. (2007). From Pictland to Alba: Scotland, 789-1070. Edinburgh University Press. ISBN: 0748612343.

[7] Martínez-Cadenas, C., López, S., Ribas, G., Flores, C., García, O., Sevilla, A., Smith-Zubiaga, I., Ibarrola-Villaba, M., Pino-Yanes Mdel, M., Gardeazabal, J., Boyano, D., García de Galdeano, A., Izagirre, N., de la Rúa, C., Alonso, S. (2013). Simultaneous purifying selection on the ancestral MC1R allele and positive selection on the melanoma-risk allele V60L in south Europeans. Molecular Biology and Evolution, 30(12):2654-65. DOI: 10.1093/molbev/mst158.

[8] Livak, L. (2010). The Jewish persona in the European imagination: A Case of Russian Literature. Stanford, California: Stanford University Press. DOI: 10.2307/j.ctvqsdt8s.

Chapter 8

Luck and Stars Constellations

[1] BBC News, are birthdays linked to luck? April 19, 2004.

[2] Ballard, J., 12 Fascinating April birthday facts that you've never heard before, GoodHousekeeping, January 25, 2021

[3-4] Zaraska, M., That bad attitude? Blame the birth month, Los Angeles Times, January 30, 2012.

[5] Söderström, U., Åman, J. and Hjern, A. (2012). Being born in Sweden increases the risk for type 1 diabetes – a study of migration of children to Sweden as a natural experiment. Acta Paediatrica, 101: 73-77

[6] Swanson, A., Scientists have discovered how the month you're born matters for your health, Washington Post, June 15, 2015.

[7] Jiang, F., Year of the Dragon, Chinahighlights, May19, 2021.

Printed in Great Britain
by Amazon